ALBERT ARRIOLA

Joe Bennett was born in Eastbourne, England. After leaving Cambridge University he taught English in several countries, including Canada, Spain, France and New Zealand, before quitting the classroom in 1998 to make his living as a writer. *Where Underpants Come From* was the 2009 Travcom Travel Book of the Year. Joe lives in Lyttelton.

DOUBLE HAPPINESS

HOW BULLSHIT WORKS

Joe Bennett

HarperCollins*Publishers*

Acknowledgment

My inadequate thanks to editor Anna Rogers, for her
expertise, patience and wisdom, but above all for giving
me courage. The faults of this book are mine alone; without
Anna they would have been far more numerous.

HarperCollins*Publishers*

First published in 2012
by HarperCollins*Publishers (New Zealand) Limited*
PO Box 1, Shortland Street, Auckland 1140

Copyright © Joe Bennett 2012

HarperCollins*Publishers*

31 View Road, Glenfield, Auckland 0627, New Zealand
Level 13, 201 Elizabeth Street, Sydney, NSW 2000, Australia
A 53, Sector 57, Noida, UP, India
77–85 Fulham Palace Road, London W6 8JB, United Kingdom
2 Bloor Street East, 20th floor, Toronto, Ontario M4W 1A8, Canada
10 East 53rd Street, New York, NY 10022, USA

National Library of New Zealand Cataloguing-in-Publication Data

Bennett, Joe, 1957-
Double happiness : how bullshit works / Joe Bennett.
ISBN 978-1-86950-957-6
1. Truthfulness and falsehood. I. Title.
177.3—dc 23

ISBN: 978 1 86950 957 6

Cover and internal design and typesetting by Springfield West

Printed by Printlink, Wellington

This publication is printed on paper pulp sourced from sustainably
grown and managed forests, using Elemental Chlorine Free (ECF)
bleaching, and printed with 100 per cent vegetable-based inks.

For Sarah and Nems in Zurich

Contents

Introduction

According to the *Oxford English Dictionary*, bullshit is a noun, a transitive verb and an intransitive verb. In other words you can talk bullshit, you can bullshit someone or you can just bullshit in general. In addition, though the *OED* doesn't mention it, the word serves as an adjective. One regularly hears of bullshit arguments, though less regularly than one should. Most arguments are bullshit. I have yet to hear bullshit used as an adverb — he spoke bullshittily — but don't write it off. The word is young and vigorous.

Again according to the *OED*, the first recorded use of bullshit with its current meaning is from a poem written in 1928 by E.E. Cummings. Cummings liked to be known as e e cummings, which is a nice example of bullshit. The refusal to use punctuation added nothing to his poetry but it did make people notice him. In the words of the ad agencies, it was a unique selling point. As a result he is better known than most of his contemporaries, a recognition that has little to do with merit.

In the poem one of Cummings' characters referred to a war as being 'a lotta bullsh*t'. I can't tell you which war but I've no doubt he was right. Bullshit has been and continues to be a feature of most wars. The reason is simple: the people who do the fighting are likely to suffer and unlikely to gain. Their leaders are in the opposite position. So those leaders need to resort to bullshit in order to persuade the fighters to fight.

The word bullshit grew up in America. I grew up in the South of England and was unfamiliar with the word until, I think, the late 1970s. The word took root because it filled a need. British English had nothing as potent. Such archaisms as poppycock and balderdash could only be used on stage or by ex-squadron leaders with vast moustaches, and otherwise there were only such innocent and gentle terms as rubbish and nonsense. The *OED* still gives these as the nearest synonyms to bullshit, but the difference is substantial.

Bullshit is nonsense, but nonsense doesn't have to be bullshit. Nonsense can be agreeable. Edward Lear's nonsense verse, for example, is fondly thought of (though not very often by me).

The Owl and the Pussycat went to sea
In a beautiful pea-green boat
They took some honey
And plenty of money
Wrapped up in a five pound note.

That's nonsense. But it isn't bullshit. Bullshit deceives.

The antithesis of bullshit is reason. Reason exposes bullshit as bullshit. So bullshit is scared of reason. In consequence, and as I shall demonstrate throughout this text, bullshit constantly dresses itself up to look like reason. It's a clear case of imitation being the sincerest flattery.

It also illustrates the accuracy of the old myth about Truth and Falsehood, who went bathing together one warm ancient day. While Truth was frolicking in the cool water, her conscience as clear as a nun's wimple, Falsehood nipped out of the pool, ran back to where they'd undressed and stole Truth's clothes. When Truth emerged dripping and discovered what Falsehood had done, she decided that she would rather wear no clothes than don Falsehood's. Hence the naked truth.

Reason has done more than any other faculty to reveal the truth. But though we enjoy the many fruits of reason, from the plough to the internet, reason itself is not popular. Indeed reason has had its back to the wall throughout human history. And from time to time it's had its back to the torturer's rack while bullshitters dressed in power tried to convince it that the sun goes round the earth or that the devil had infested it or that the supreme leader was a good man or whatever species of bullshit served the current needs of the bullshitters. Reason generally prevails in the end because it can be shown to be right, but it does not do so easily. And every bit of ground it wins is constantly in danger of being repopulated by bullshit.

Bullshit has always been with us. But as a result of the proliferation of media in the last century or so, there is now more of it than ever, and it is harder than ever to avoid. We are awash with bullshit, drowning in it. It assails us constantly, from walls and pages, from speakers and screens. It has become so accepted a part of the human landscape that bullshitters cannot merely make a living from bullshit, and achieve power and prestige and wealth from bullshit, they can even win prizes for it. Unironic prizes.

The five standard journalistic interrogatives are who, what, why, where and how.

Who bullshits? It is easier to list the people who don't. One, of course, is my sainted mother. The other, obviously, is you, the reader. The rest of us, to varying degrees, are guilty.

What is bullshit? It is the wilful use of at least partial dishonesty.

Why do people bullshit? In order to gain an advantage of some sort, in the form of money or power. And since money is essentially an expression of power, the nub of the matter is that a bullshitter seeks some sort of power over the bullshittee, most commonly commercial power, or political power, or religious power.

Where do people bullshit? Everywhere they can. If we in the developed world were to strip all bullshit from our streets, our screens, our papers and our airwaves we would barely recognize the civilization we were left with.

How do people bullshit? Answering that question is the aim of this book. I mean to unpack examples of bullshit from New Zealand and elsewhere in order to expose the techniques they employ. These techniques are surprisingly few and surprisingly simple.

There are two possible outcomes of this process. One is that the bullshitters will realize that the game is up. They will emerge en masse from their offices and their mansions and their palaces to confess their sins. A huge weight will fall from their shoulders as the politicians, the ad agencies, the experts, the pope, the motivational speakers, the mullahs, the marketers and all the unholy rest of them come forward over the brow of the hill like the von Trapp children, holding hands and singing. Never more, they sing, shall we bullshit. It will be a fine moment.

The other possibility, a remote one, but there nevertheless, is that this book will make no difference. The bullshitters will continue to bullshit the bullshittees, using the same tired old methods. And if so, well, I will have said my piece.

1

The contempt of conflation

As I begin this book, the newspapers are dominated by Libya, where Colonel Gaddafi is coming to the end of forty years of dictatorship. He is still urging his few remaining supporters to fight, to 'drive the rats back to the sewers they came from', but in the best traditions of cornered dictators, he is doing this urging via the radio from some unidentified bunker. Inevitably he has announced that he will never flee his beloved Libya, that he prefers to die like a martyr on his native soil. In other words he's planning to flee.

I could easily, therefore, begin a discussion of bullshit with Libya, but I choose to begin on Cheapside in London one morning last summer, because that's when I decided to write this book.

Cheapside is a short street that runs between St Paul's Cathedral and the City of London, so in a discussion of bullshit I could have fun at either end. But I made the decision about halfway along, outside a bank near Tesco Metro.

It was rush hour. Men and women scurried to work, talking into cell phones, drinking coffee from paper cups with lids on, the sort of lids that used to be given only to toddlers. No one paid any attention to the bank. Its window showed a life-size image of Lewis Hamilton, the racing driver. He was wearing his white racing-driver overalls with the quasimodic hump at the back to protect his priceless spinal cord in the event of a crash. The overalls were dotted with the names of companies that had paid to be there.

He carried his racing helmet under his arm, so as to reveal his pleasant face. His racial provenance has given him full lips, good teeth and skin the colour of fresh engine oil, youth has given him health and cheerfulness, and his skill at driving fast cars has given him wealth and fame. In other words, the bugger's got the lot.

There were a few words on the poster, purporting to have issued from Mr Hamilton's smiling lips. The words were: 'Together we are Santander.'

Santander is a port in the north of Spain but here the name denotes the Bank of Santander, the owners of the window. In recent years this bank has expanded far beyond the city of its birth, especially in the UK. It has acquired several businesses, including Abbey National, a building society, which had in turn had previously acquired Bradford & Bingley, another building society.

It is worth digressing for a moment to consider Bradford & Bingley. Naturally enough they used to be what their name suggests, a building society based in Bradford and Bingley. Such a name would have reassured cagey Yorkshire folk that their building society was strictly local and had nothing to do with the flash Harrys down south. But Bradford & Bingley became ambitious. It started to consort with every Tom, Dick and flash Harry it could find and by doing so it became the biggest mortgage lender in the country. Though it continued to call itself Bradford & Bingley it now had branches all over the country. And in 2008 it went bust.

The British Government stepped in and nationalized the mortgage side of the business. It sold the rest to Abbey National. Then Santander bought Abbey National.

Thus the bank found itself doing business a long way from Santander and facing the problem of being almost unknown to the great British public. To overcome that problem it sponsored motor racing, and hired Lewis Hamilton to be the face of the bank.

At first glance banking has nothing to do with motor racing. At second glance, it has even less. Where banking requires prudence, motor racing requires daring. Banking is dull and safe (or is supposed to be), motor racing thrilling and dangerous. Where bankers must make provision against disaster, conscious always that they are the trusted guardians of the money that people love, racing drivers operate on the screaming edge of traction. Banking eschews risk. Motor racing courts it. Motor racing is death or glory stuff, littered with crashes. The success of a bank is dependent on its never crashing. Banks prosper by steady accumulation, whereas in motor racing the commonest outcome is loss. But the victories, though rare, are moments of huge ephemeral glory, celebrated by priapic plumes of wasted champagne.

In short, were there a list of activities most dissimilar to retail banking, motor racing would be near the top. Which is, of course, precisely why

Santander hired Lewis Hamilton. They hoped to make their sexless business seem sexy. They hoped that when the public saw or heard the name Santander, the image that rose to mind would not be of a dull bank, indistinguishable from every other dull bank, apart from its additional disadvantage of being foreign, but rather of the glamour and thrills of motor racing and a sexy young English hero.

The bullshit involved is the technique of conflation. It is simple to the point of crudeness. If you have a product or a service, or an idea or a belief, that you wish to foist upon the world, you conflate it with something the world already knows and likes. The two things do not have to be in any way related. Indeed the more distinct they are, the more striking and memorable the effect. The idea is that if you conflate the two things with persistence, the positive emotions aroused by the known thing transfer by a sort of osmosis onto the previously unknown thing, the thing you have to foist.

Conflation is a fundamental of bullshit. It comes in numerous forms and I shall return to it repeatedly. But for the moment I wish merely to point out that it is also fundamental to dog training.

I am not much good at dog training. All my dogs turn into the same dog, one who is good-natured, affable and part-time obedient. The part of the time when the dog is obedient is when it doesn't need to be. When I do need it to be, I might as well whistle Jesus.

Nevertheless I have read several books about training dogs. The nub of the matter is behavioural conditioning. And the nub of behavioural conditioning is conflation. You conflate the things you want the dog to do with good consequences. So, for example, if the dog sits when asked to sit, it gets a biscuit. The dog rapidly understands the pattern 'If x, then y', which is about as far as dog reasoning goes. Sitting and biscuits become yoked together in his simple mind. Just as the bank of Santander and Lewis Hamilton become yoked in ours.

There is, however, one vital distinction. If the dog sits, it does get a biscuit. If you open an account with Santander, you don't get Lewis Hamilton.

2

The conflation of kings, despots and similar buggers

Gaddafi didn't manage to flee his beloved country. It seems that his beloved countrymen hauled him out of a sewage pipe and shot him. Gaddafi's forty years of absolute rule and his refusal to step down illustrate the old truth that despots like being despots, just as kings like being kings. Very few ever abdicate. Almost everywhere throughout human history, the only way to get rid of a despot or monarch has been to wait for him to die or to kill him. Though in either case he was likely to be succeeded by his son. Breaking that dynastic pattern has been the great triumph of democracy.

The reason kings like to be kings is not far to seek. They get to eat and drink well at the expense of their subjects. Those subjects also have sons and daughters whom kings get to enjoy, according to taste. And kings can make the rules, fun rules like taxation, to which they are not themselves subject but from which they profit. Gaddafi is said to have stashed away billions.

The bullet or bullets that did for Gaddafi demonstrate, if demonstration were needed, that he was a frail mortal organism like every one of his subjects. That same fact was even more vividly illustrated by the capture of Saddam Hussein a few years back. When they hauled him from his literal hole in the ground, he looked like a park bench wino. The film of him undergoing a check-up from an army doctor with latex gloves and a tongue depressor was close to pitiful. It was hard to square this wild-eyed bearded wretch with the bloody tyrant.

That rulers are little different from their subjects is, for the rulers, an awkward truth. It is easier to rule if your subjects revere you, but they need a reason to do so. The qualities that often distinguish despots, such as brutality, selfishness and a pathological lust for power, are not endearing ones. So the despots need to suggest better things about themselves. And to this end they have always engaged in various forms of bullshit, one of which is conflation.

But they have to be careful. By definition, a king is the apex of his society. So if he were to set about conflating himself with, say, the Lewis Hamilton of his day, in the hope that some of Mr Hamilton's handsome heroism would rub off on him, he'd run the risk of implying the superiority of Mr Hamilton. In which case it would make more sense to crown King Lewis the First.

The conflationary figure a king requires is someone or something held in esteem by his subjects but not itself eligible for the crown. Wild animals sometimes serve. Gaddafi — what a cornily traditional dictator he proved to be, but then again they nearly all do — liked to be known as the Lion of Africa (or of the Desert, depending on his mood). He was, of course, no more noticeably leonine than jolly old Richard the Lionheart, who periodically set off on crusades to smite the heathen in the name of a loving god, just as lions do. (The heathen, understandably, was just as eager to smite back in the name of his own loving god.)

But although the animal kingdom can supply ferocity and athleticism, it struggles to furnish examples of wisdom, or caring leadership. For these the conflationary leader reaches into the grave, where he has a choice of millions of dead people, none of whom is a threat. They can't take the throne, and they have established reputations which they are too dead to ruin by putting a hand in the till or up a chorister's cassock.

If you were asked to scour the legions of dead for a corpse with whom to compare George W. Bush, it might not occur to you to finger Thomas Jefferson. It did occur to George, or at least to his speechwriter.

Here's the wrap-up of George's rousing inaugural address of 2001.

Much time has passed since Jefferson arrived for his inauguration. The years and changes accumulate. But the themes of this day he would know: our nation's grand story of courage and its simple dream of dignity.

Never tiring, never yielding, never finishing, we renew that purpose today, to make our country more just and generous, to affirm the dignity of our lives and every life.

This work continues. This story goes on. And

an angel still rides in the whirlwind and directs
this storm.

God bless you all, and God bless America.

There are various forms of bullshit at work here,
but for the moment note the effect of conflation. By
implication rather than assertion, George becomes
Jefferson reincarnate, an almost disembodied figure
in the grand pageant of history, sanctified by the past,
driven by lofty principles, an emblem of all that is
good about the USA, a vessel crammed with virtues
and with no interest whatsoever in oil companies.

George W. chose not to conflate himself with his
father George H.W. This is unsurprising. Father,
however, did choose to conflate himself with his
son. He did it at birth by saddling him with the
same name, thus performing the most ancient act
of conflation, the dynastic one. Like father, like son.
It is a conflation with more hope of being justified
than any other. Son does, after all, get Dad's DNA,
so genetically he's a chip off the old block. But that
chip is not only contaminated by Mum, it is further
buggered around by nurture.

Let's say Dad was raised in the traditional log cabin
of hardship. He will often credit the virtues he learned
in the log cabin for his subsequent rise to power,

and to some degree he may be right. But because of Dad's success his son will never see the inside of a log cabin. He will know only the detached house of prosperity. And however earnestly Dad may try to instil the log-cabin virtues, he'll struggle because his son will have it easy. And there is a long tradition of sons who have it easy becoming wastrels.

If you look, say, at the sweep of Chinese history a wave pattern emerges. Every dynasty began with an energetic rebel warlord who seized power. The next son or two enlarged and consolidated the empire. But then came sons who had a taste for corruption and self-indulgence. At which point there arose a new energetic rebel warlord, and a new dynastic wave began.

Nevertheless the conflation of son with father is a staple of despotic bullshit, stimulated partly by the dynastic urge but also, one suspects, by Dad's fear that anyone outside the family is more likely to be disloyal. So Gaddafi's sons were groomed for succession and given sinecures like Head of Torture. Ditto Saddam Hussein's. Most blatant of all is the chubby chops who has assumed the throne of North Korea, in succession to his father and grandfather. The business of conflating the new dear leader with the former dear leaders has already begun.

Drive anywhere in Dubai and you will see spectacular car crashes. But if you can take your eyes off the exploits of those drivers who have yet to crash, you will see billboards the size of houses, featuring an image of Dubai's ruler, Sheik Mohammed bin Rashid al Maktoum. He is standing in the desert wearing the whitest of dishdashas and a headcloth affixed with a camel halter, as has become the uniform of top Arabs. He is staring nobly beyond the horizon in a manner that even the earliest Hollywood promoters would have found a bit overdone, and on either side of him are his two sons doing the same thing. The words across the top, 'Our Visionary Leaders'.

Sheik Mohammed is a popular and by and large successful ruler. It could even be argued that he has been visionary. But by conflating the sons with the father before those sons have had a chance to prove their worth or lack of it, the ruling family is doing all it can to establish a self-perpetuating dynasty.

New Zealand is neither a tyranny nor an autocracy. Yet the unwarranted propaganda of conflation goes on here as it does everywhere. Through the winter of 2011, for example, it must have been tough being All Black captain Richie McCaw. Every time he turned round who should he find clapping a hand on his shoulder and smiling for the camera but Prime

Minister John Key. The Rugby World Cup was held in New Zealand and Mr Key did all he could to conflate himself with the national team and with Richie McCaw in particular. Yet Mr Key's contribution to the team was precisely the same as yours or mine. His association with the All Blacks differed little from Lewis Hamilton's with the Bank of Santander.

In his defence, John Key was only maintaining a tradition. His predecessor, Helen Clark, did not at first glance seem a likely rugby fan. Yet on one occasion during her reign she whipped her motorcade to speeds in excess of 160 kph in a bid to reach a test match on time.

Mr Key staked a lot on the Rugby World Cup. It proved a good bet. The All Blacks won the cup by a narrow margin. And a month later Mr Key won a general election by a rather larger one.

(As I write the New Zealand cricket team is being thrashed by South Africa. The prime minister has not, as far as I am aware, attended.)

3

Kings and the big boy

So, rulers conflate themselves with animals, dead people, offspring and World Cup-winning rugby teams for the purpose of cementing power. But by far the commonest and most effective conflationary partner of rulers throughout the history of human civilization has been god.

Gods come in various forms but certain qualities are common to pretty well all of them: they are immortal; they are to be feared and revered; they are unknowable and unpredictable; they are powerful beyond the scope of mere mortals to resist; and they are liable to do spectacularly nasty things to you if you cross them, not only in this life but also, and this is particularly useful from the bullshitter's point of view, when you are dead. The nub of the matter is that it is seriously unwise to vex gods and suicidal to rebel against them. Which is why kings of all varieties have made every effort to conflate themselves with gods since human society began.

Egyptian pharaohs, Chinese emperors, Inca overlords, indeed just about all bosses everywhere, have striven to make themselves indistinguishable from, or at the least a very close associate of, him upstairs. Quite a lot of them, I'd imagine, have even come to believe their own bullshit. 'Cry God for Harry, England and St George.' Church, state and king, conflated into a single entity.

Nor is the conflation of monarchs with gods a quaint relic of a superstitious past. The Japanese, for example, were probably the most committed troops fighting the Second World War. Some of them famously kept at it for decades. Their cause was the emperor, Hirohito, whom ritual and tradition had rendered a demigod.

Several twentieth-century regimes claimed to have abolished god and established a secular society. They did no such thing. Rather they took conflation to its maximal and logical conclusion, whereby ruler and god became the same thing. And that thing was the ruler. He was god on earth.

Images of that leader — Stalin, Mao, Kim Il Sung — became as ubiquitous as god is meant to be. The leader watched over all people at all times and he knew all things. His little book of sayings became the new scripture. He required utter devotion. The flattery he received was indistinguishable, at least in form, from religious worship. Stalin, who is among the top flight of mass murderers in human history, was called 'the great gardener of human happiness', whose 'unlimited love for his people' made him the 'standard bearer of universal peace'. You'll find similar lines in *Hymns Ancient and Modern*.

When Rick Santorum, who is a Catholic, was still in the race to become the Republican candidate for the American presidency, he stated that a speech given by President Kennedy stressing the need to separate church and state made him, Santorum, 'want to throw up'. You could hear the Vatican cheering.

I am not accusing Santorum of conflating himself with god — not yet at any rate. But if he had become president, and if he had somehow achieved his aim of returning church and state to the same fold, it would have been a retreat for our species. Back we'd have gone to the days of conflating policy with god's will. God's will is incontrovertible. To go against it is to blaspheme. Blasphemy is a crime. Hello, dictatorship.

(If Santorum, by the way, had done a straw poll around the world he would have found many who would share his point of view. They would include, to take just two examples, the Taleban in Afghanistan, where the Americans have long been waging a war, and the clerics in charge of Iran, where the Americans look likely to wage one soon.)

Church and state is the oldest and most effective power combo in the history of human affairs. It is our default setting. Chief and juju man, monarch and priest, royalty and mumbo jumbo, awe and reverence, god and king. It's easy to see what the chief gets out of it: god on his side. And it's equally easy to see what the juju man gets out of it: the chief on his side. The relationship is symbiotic. Each party is bolstered by the other in a self-contained reflexive arrangement that, over the centuries, has proved the most effective way of keeping the mob quiet. Fear, reverence and obedience — and unlimited sums of money — all of it achieved through conflation.

I recently watched black and white footage of the coronation of Queen Elizabeth II. The event took place in god's house. Bishops in tall hats flocked around the princess like an elderly chapter of the Ku Klux Klan. The most vital bit of the ceremony was obscured from the television cameras by a little gazebo, because it was simply too sacred. Everything was explained in reverential whispers by an early Dimbleby, who cooed over sacred artefacts and chunks of ritual that had been sanctified by centuries of tradition.

Only they weren't sacred. They may have been old but age doesn't confer divine provenance. Trace any item used in the service back far enough, any word spoken or any gesture made, and it will be found to have originated with some king, priest or courtier deciding to use it for the first time, probably as a means of wowing the peasants. None of it was ordained. All of it was deliberately conceived to conflate the monarch with the big cheese. And, simultaneously, to conflate the big cheese's church with the monarchy.

A coronation ceremony may fulfil a tribal need. It clearly tugs at a string in the credulous human heart. But that does not stop it at the same time being riddled to its core with deliberate and manipulative conflationary bullshit.

4

The slither of expertise

Hong Kong airport, like all international airports, abounds in posh shops. Single, duckling-coloured sweaters are folded and lit for display like museum exhibits. Prices are indicated by blocks of movable type on little Scrabble racks. Most of the blocks say zero. The shop assistants are all young Hong Kongese, slim, polite, bilingual at the least, impeccably groomed and smooth of skin. Their customers are, by and large, past it.

The past-it customers, especially the female ones,

would like to be young, slim and smooth of skin. So the shops offer them tiny bottles of anti-aging cream at enormous prices. Or bottles of liquor to help them forget.

The men, meanwhile, are offered accoutrements — most prominently, watches. One shop is fronted by a huge ad, showing George Clooney at the helm of a motorboat. He is steering it across a Mediterranean harbour suggestive of wealth and exclusivity — Antibes, perhaps, or Monaco. His hair is unruffled, his clothes are casual and his forearms bare to the blessing of the sun except for a watch that looks to weigh about a pound and a half. 'George Clooney', it says, 'chooses Rolex.'

The obvious conflationary process that the ad tries to exploit can be expressed more or less as follows:

George Clooney is suave, rich and irritatingly sexually successful.

George Clooney chooses Rolex.

Therefore if I choose Rolex, I too will be suave, rich and irritatingly sexually successful.

Which doesn't, when put that baldly, seem too likely. And it seems even less likely when you consider that the following sequence has the same logical pattern:

My neighbour is a gay chartered accountant.

My neighbour wears brown shoes.

Therefore if I wear brown shoes I will become a gay chartered accountant.

The word 'chooses' is curious. One suspects that it was Rolex rather than Mr Clooney that did the choosing. They thought that Mr Clooney would make a nice mascot for Rolex so they went to see his agent bearing gifts, including a watch or two, no doubt, and perhaps a little cheque to compensate for the inconvenience of flying to Antibes for a photo shoot. Choosing did not come into it.

But even if it did, even if Mr Clooney does choose Rolex, and even if he is so fond of his watch that he sent the company of his own free will the photograph of himself in his boat and told them they were welcome to use it as promotion in any way they wished and without cost as a token of his gratitude for their having made such an excellent and reliable timepiece, it still doesn't explain why Mr Clooney's choice of Rolex should matter to us. For George Clooney is an actor. He is not an horologist.

If The Suave and Sexy Acting School of New York were to post an advertisement saying 'George Clooney reckons we're good', it would be reasonable to take notice because George knows a thing or two about acting. But there is no evidence that he knows anything about watches. The ad merely depends on us subconsciously transferring his expertise in one field to another entirely unrelated field. Which is like taking Lewis Hamilton's advice on banking because he drives well, or Albert Einstein's on personal grooming because he's good at physics.

Of course the ad does not explicitly transfer the expertise. It merely opens the door for the consumer to do so. And should the consumer walk through that door and buy a watch in the vague hope that it will bring him fame, good looks, a motorboat and ineffable sexual charm, then that is his decision. Caveat, in other words, emptor. And at the least he'll end up owning a nice watch. The ad may have encouraged a minor self-deception but there is no great harm done. Such a happy outcome, however, does not always stem from this form of bullshit. Sometimes the emptor walks through the door and is ruined.

Colin Meads captained the All Blacks in the days of amateur heroism. He's getting on a bit now but he still embodies certain qualities that are part of New Zealand's image of itself — hard-working, unquestionably masculine, uncomplaining, rural, and terrifyingly good at rugby. So he's a popular bloke.

A few years ago he appeared on television promoting a finance company. Finance companies are risky banks. They charge higher rates of interest to borrowers because they tend to lend on ventures that the banks have turned down. And they pay correspondingly higher rates of interest to depositors.

Meads expressed the opinion that an outfit called Provincial Finance was 'solid as', which is rural Kiwi-speak for 'you can't go wrong'. But you could go wrong. In the credit crisis a few years later Provincial Finance went as wrong as it is possible to go. It went bust. Depositors lost millions. And those who'd put money in because Colin Meads said it was solid as, were victims of the bullshit of transferred expertise. For although Colin Meads in his day was an expert at rucking, mauling, snaffling line-outs and flinging opponents aside, all of which added greatly to the joy of a nation, none of those things qualified him to read a balance sheet, assess risk or offer financial advice. Some people lost their life savings.

Rugby league in New Zealand is the poor cousin of rugby union. It's a famously tough game played by big men who bang into each other with scary ferocity. It is most popular in the impoverished urban quarters where there are heavy concentrations of Pacific Islanders and Maori, the perpetual underclass of this country.

If you aspired to become a hero of rugby league

you probably wouldn't choose to be called Stacey. Nor would you choose to be 5 foot 5. But Stacey Jones overcame the apparent handicap of his name and the actual handicap of his size to become one of New Zealand's best league players. In the process he showed himself to be, as far as it is possible to tell from media coverage, a modest and delightful man, unaffected by fame and adulation. He retired a while back to glowing acclamation from all who knew him and even greater incandescence from those who didn't.

A few months later Stacey Jones popped up on billboards, smiling in front of an improbably clean and modern office. Behind him stood a Pacific Island girl who was also smiling. Stacey was plugging Instant Finance, an outfit whose slogan is 'Helping Kiwis get ahead'. It specializes in small personal loans to the hard-up, the sort of people with large families and low-wage jobs who run out of cash before pay day, the sort of people, in other words, who are likely to follow rugby league. Lending money to the poor has rarely been seen as an heroic or virtuous business, so it is understandable that Instant Finance should wish to conflate itself with someone perceived as a virtuous hero. But, once again, anyone who borrows money from Instant Finance on Stacey's say-so, is transferring expertise. The borrower is implicitly assuming that a good footballer is therefore a good budgetary adviser. He may be or he may not be. The error lies in the word therefore.

About the same time that Colin Meads was promoting Provincial Finance, another company, Hanover Finance, was using Richard Long, a former television newsreader. In doing so they were exploiting, or at least encouraging people to commit, a remarkable double transference of expertise.

The two qualities required of a television newsreader are an appearance that isn't actively repellent and the ability to read out loud nicely. He or she is just a messenger. It is recognized as bad practice to shoot a messenger. But it is equally bad practice to revere one. Yet it happens all the time.

Because news stories are, at least in theory, authoritative, impartial and trustworthy, those qualities tend to rub off on the person who reads them out. In other words, the news gatherer's expertise is transferred onto the news presenter. So when Mr Long retired he took with him a conflationary aura of detached, almost Solomonic wisdom. It was this transferred expertise that Hanover Finance bought, in the hope that potential investors would transfer it for a second time, and see the Solomon of journalism as the Solomon, therefore, of financial analysis. They did. The ads ran for a long time, which presumably indicates that they sucked the money in. Then Hanover Finance, like Provincial Finance, went bung and most of the money vanished.

Deconstructing commercial advertising to reveal its false and grasping heart is like shooting fish in a barrel. But advertising is so fundamental to our way of life, so accepted and so ubiquitous, that I think it worth doing. And besides, shooting fish in a barrel isn't easy. The water's dark, fish move with shimmying speed, and refraction is likely to upset your aim. What I'm trying to do is to empty the barrel, smash it to bits and tip the fish onto the grass in order to have a good look at them. And once you've had a clear view of these fish you can't help spotting them in different barrels. They get everywhere, the slippery little buggers.

For example, it is now well over a year since the earthquake in Christchurch that killed close to 200 people. The initial effect was like the kicking of an ants' nest. People scurried in panic, then set to work patching things up. Gradually the frenzy subsided and people are now looking long rather than short. There has been a commission of inquiry into all the earthquake deaths to which many engineers and building owners have been summoned to justify their actions. They have not enjoyed the experience. Though no blame has been specifically attached, they have felt very much under scrutiny.

In the wake of that inquiry a number of buildings that had survived the major quakes and the 10,000 or so aftershocks have suddenly been closed, causing many people both inconvenience and financial hardship. No one wants to be found culpable, so they have become hyper-cautious.

The local paper ran a substantial article on this subject. It focused on the opinion of a man whose wife died in a collapsed building. He held the view that all buildings potentially vulnerable to further quakes should be abandoned until rendered safe. Of course one sympathizes with the man concerned. He has suffered grievously. This makes him an authority on the subject of grief. But not on risk. There is no reason to believe that his opinion on what level of risk is acceptable is any wiser or better informed than yours or mine. Indeed you could reasonably argue that his experience will have distorted his view of things. The point, once again, is the illegitimate transfer of expertise.

It's common in politics too. Apart from being actors, what do the following have in common: Robert de Niro, Eddie Murphy, Jennifer Aniston, Ben Affleck, Morgan Freeman, Matt Damon and the ever-present George Clooney? The answer, according to an article I have just found on the internet, is that they all publicly endorsed Barack Obama in his 2008 bid for the presidency. (I did as well, as it happens, but for some reason my name was left out of the article.)

Most Americans vote either Democrat or Republican throughout their adult life. So every election is decided by the comparatively few who swing. These are the people any aspiring politician needs to persuade, and celebrity endorsements are part of the process.

Donald Trump, for example, came down on the side of Republican Mitt Romney. Mitt was thrilled. There was television coverage of Mitt pumping Trump's hand and grinning like a chimp. Quite why Mitt should have been so pleased, I cannot say. If I needed a little extra something to persuade me that Mitt Romney is iffy, Trump's endorsement would do nicely. That the Obama supporters I listed are all actors, and therefore skilled at dressing up and pretending, ought to make them less trustworthy than most people. But it clearly doesn't. Their skills in the field of entertainment are presumed, subconsciously, to bleed into the political field.

Two other names on the 2008 list of Obama supporters were Ethel Kennedy, widow of Bobby, and Warren Buffett, the 'legendary investor' (and that phrase can wait for attention). On the face of it, these endorsements would seem to carry more weight. The woman carries a political aura, the man an economic one.

But again the impression is inexact. Mrs Kennedy's political experience was a long time ago and at one remove, and as the mother of eleven children she presumably had little time for taking part in her husband's political life. And since his death she has played no part in politics other than to endorse candidates from time to time and host the occasional fundraising dinner. Her political experience hardly merits the word expertise. Warren Buffett's expertise consists of spotting companies he believes will prosper and putting his money into them. And though that is undoubtedly a form of expertise, it carries no whiff of political awareness or policy analysis. So endorsements from these two are of little more value rationally than those of the acting troupe.

Spectacularly absent from the list of Obama's endorsers are the names of people well qualified to judge the matter. There are no Harvard professors of public policy. No theoretical political scientists.

No moral philosophers. I would imagine that many such people did endorse Obama and vote for him, but their names have not found their way into the public domain. The difference between them and the luminaries is one thing only, the fairy dust of fame. Sprinkle it and reason wilts.

5

The god of post hoc bull

The end of winter approached. The people gathered at the sacred site. Onto the stone they hauled the struggling goat. It bleated piteously. The shaman or high priest or whoever currently held the direct line to the goddess raised his blade to the sky, muttered an incantation, then slit the animal's throat. The hooves kicked for a few seconds, then fell limp. An acolyte held a bowl of beaten metal to catch the still warm blood. One by one the people filed past to dip a finger and smear their foreheads.

The beast was butchered and roasted on a fire made with wood from a sacred tree, and the best cuts of meat were offered to the goddess. When she didn't turn up to eat them, the shaman did. There was no point in wasting good goat.

In this way, the goddess of fertility, or spring or sun or weather in general or any of the other things the people relied on but could not control, was appeased. Within weeks, days even, the air warmed and crops sprouted. The sacrifice had worked. And the tribe had fallen for the oldest and most persistent variety of bullshit known to our species, the fallacy known as post hoc ergo propter hoc, or after this and therefore on account of this.

The fallacy lies in the word therefore. The only relationship between killing the goat and the arrival of spring is that one preceded the other. There is no evidence that one caused the other. It would be as legitimate to argue that because I bought two pillows on 10 September 2001, which I did, at Briscoes in Salisbury Street, I caused terrorists to fly planes into the World Trade Centre the following day. A temporal relationship is not, of necessity, a causal relationship.

But it is easy to see how goat sacrifices came about. We are all guilty, I suspect, of equally superstitious and shoddy thinking. As a young cricketer I always used to put my left pad on first (and still do on the rare occasions I play). It would be bad luck not to.

What I sought, I suppose, was some sort of consolation, however imaginary, in a situation that scared me. I desperately wanted to score runs — I was absurdly keen — but there were forces out there that I could not control, primary among which were fast bowlers. I felt I needed Lady Luck on my side so I invented a ritual to propitiate her. In other words I started a private religion, inventing and personifying an imaginary power, then doing what I could to please her in the hope that she would favour me. For left pad read goat.

I can no longer recall how I developed the superstition. Presumably I made a conscious decision one day to don the left pad first and then scored runs. And on the post hoc principle I persisted.

Occasionally thereafter I scored a century. Far more often I didn't. The obvious conclusion to draw was that putting the left pad on first made no difference. But I never put that to the test by reaching for the right pad first. I didn't dare. I was a bright child and had been taught the scientific method at school, the application of which would have banished the left-pad superstition to the pavilion rubbish bin. But in a business that mattered to me I preferred the warm comfort of misplaced belief to the cool demonstrability of reason. The human tragedy writ very small.

The post hoc fallacy retains a grip on our minds and wallets. Today's shamans are the direct descendants, effectively unchanged, of the goat slaughterer. They rely every bit as much as he did on their adherents preferring post hoc hope over rational sense. Consider, for example, the pope before the present one, the charismatic John Paul II. Frail but indomitable, heroic yet humble, he resembled an elderly, male Princess Di. The faithful flocked. When his body lay in state the queue of mourners was apparently visible from space. This was excellent for the church and they were understandably keen to capitalize on it. So they put the dead John Paul on the fast track to sainthood.

The church has a protocol for making saints, though where they got it from and how they justify it I have no idea. But they like to put it about that it is a rigorous business. You can't have just anyone being canonized. One of the requirements is that the would-be saint has to be shown to have worked a miracle or two. These are generally medical. Two have been ascribed to the intervention of the late pope.

The first was the complete cure of Sister Marie Simon-Pierre, a French nun who had been suffering from Parkinson's disease. Her sisters in the convent prayed to John Paul and suddenly she was cured. (Or may have been. It is not entirely certain that she had Parkinson's, nor is it entirely certain that if she did, it has gone.) The other miracle happened to a Polish boy with kidney cancer. He was so sick he could barely walk. But he was taken to visit the tomb of the former pope and shortly afterwards he, too, got better. And of course I am pleased for him, just as I am pleased for Sister Marie Simon-Pierre, if she is cured, and if indeed she was sick in the first place.

In order to determine whether these events should be considered miracles, the Vatican appoints both a theological and a medical panel. These panels consist of intelligent human beings who debate matters with great seriousness. Yet not one of them ever thinks, or perhaps dares, to point out the post hoc fallacy.

It may be true that the sisters prayed to John Paul and that shortly afterwards Sister Marie Simon-Pierre was cured. But the only demonstrable relationship between the two events is that one preceded the other. There is not a scrap of evidence that one caused the other. The same is self-evidently true of the Polish boy's trip to the tomb and his recovery.

Yet there is abundant evidence, overwhelming evidence, of the absence of a causal relationship. That evidence is the millions, perhaps billions, of prayers biffed at John Paul to no effect whatsoever. That evidence is the thousands of sick nuns who've both prayed and been prayed for but have then died. That evidence is the stream of sick children who have visited and continue to visit John Paul's tomb and wake up the following morning still sick. Has John Paul got something against these mites?

You must almost admire the devotion of the Catholic church to its dogma and its insistence on defying reason and affirming hocus pocus based on a demonstrable fallacy, a fallacy that was identified and named by the evolving human mind several thousand years ago, but that continues to thrive like a goat-blessed crop.

6

Holy water

The word infomercial is transparent bullshit. Infomercials are screened during the inexpensive hours when only the sad, lonely or drunk are watching television, so the advertisers can afford to make their ads longer. Thus they gain a resemblance to marginally more informative programmes to which viewers might be inclined to give some credence.

The same bullshit lies behind the word advertorial. It means an advertisement that consists mainly of text, rather than catchy slogans or emotive images.

Thus it superficially resembles a newspaper editorial, that sonorous opinion piece supposedly emanating from the editor's throne itself. To stress that illusory resemblance it has appropriated half the word.

The following is taken from an advertorial for the Homeopathy Centre in Christchurch. The homeopathist begins, encouragingly, by confronting the truth. ' "Most conventional scientists and physicians have expressed scepticism," says owner Elisabeth Fink.' (They've actually done a bit more than express scepticism, but let that be.)

Homeopaths were often labelled 'quacks' and positive treatment outcomes were usually regarded as the placebo effect ... [but] when we see the positive results of homeopathy on animals, no one can argue that it is due to placebo effect ... One of the centre's clients came in about her sick dog, who had developed a fever and a hard swollen gland on his neck. The vet thought his problem was caused by kennel cough vaccination and prescribed antibiotics, which made no difference after three days ...

Within a few hours of the first homeopathic prescription given, he started eating and looking happier. The next remedy brought the fever down the following day; still the gland remained swollen, which called for another prescription.

A couple of days later, I found out the gland had shrunk down and the dog was almost back to normal.

This is bullshit triple distilled. For it is not only a post hoc argument, it is also a prejudiced post hoc argument and a selective post hoc argument.

It is a post hoc argument because although the homeopathic prescription preceded the dog's recovery there is no evidence that it caused the dog's recovery. It would be just as valid to claim that the dog recovered because it had travelled to the homeopathist's by car or because I'd been out buying pillows again. Both these events would bear the same temporal relationship to the dog's recovery.

It is a prejudiced post hoc argument because the author has prejudged the truth. Because she is a homeopathist she concludes that the dog was cured by homeopathy rather than by the car journey or my pillow purchase. She has her answer in advance and is delighted to see that the facts can be interpreted to fit it.

And it is a selective post hoc argument because she selects one of the possible causes of the dog's recovery while ignoring others. It is indeed possible that the dog was cured by giving it water that contains no trace of the alleged curative substance (which is how homeopathy is supposed to operate). But it is also possible that the dog would have got better anyway. Animals recover from all sorts of maladies without medical intervention, just as we do from the common cold, and indeed from the majority of ailments that don't kill us. That's the immune system for you.

It is further possible — and may I be daring and suggest it's just a little more likely? — that the dog was cured by the vet's antibiotics. But I can't prove my case any more than the homeopathist can prove hers.

If either of us wanted to prove it we would have to do some trials. We would need a statistically significant number of similarly sick dogs and we would need to apply one treatment to some of them and one to others and no treatment at all to yet others and see how they all turned out. Which is, of course, crudely put, the scientific method, and it is also precisely what was done with the vet's lovely antibiotics before they were allowed anywhere near Fido. Not so the homeopathist's potions.

What the homeopathist ignores in her whingeing about the scepticism of 'conventional scientists and physicians' is that if homeopathy could be shown to work under such rigorous testing, those same scientists and physicians would cease their scepticism on the instant and would hug the homeopathist to their cynical bosoms. For that is how science works: from the evidence to the conclusion.

What the homeopathist also ignores is that vets and doctors like to effect cures. It's both what they're in the job for and how they make their living. And if they could cure sick dogs with the application of a little distilled water, they'd do it. Think, if nothing else, of the money they'd save. Homeopathists sell holy water. It has the same cure rate as the shade of old John Paul.

The headline of the advertorial was 'Homeopathy results: animals don't lie'. Actually animals do. When I'm fishing I sometimes disturb paradise ducks with a brood of ducklings. A parent duck will immediately pretend to have a broken wing. As I continue up the river the duck stays ahead of me, splashing, squawking and feigning the injury. It can do this for a mile or more. And as far as the duck is concerned the ruse works because I keep following it.

The duck appears to have fallen for the post hoc fallacy. It faked an injury. I followed it upstream. Therefore I followed it upstream because it faked an injury, whereas I actually moved upstream only because that's what you do when fly-fishing. But the duck isn't thinking like that. The duck isn't thinking at all. It's just acting on instinct. It has no choice. And that instinct evolved by a more rigorous process of trial and error than any homeopathy cure has ever undergone, the process of evolution. Ducks that lured predators away tended to succeed at reproducing. Ducks that didn't didn't. So deceptive ducks thrived and non-deceptive ducks died out. Evolution never cares why something works. It is incapable of caring. It is a blind unconscious process. But it is ruthlessly efficient. Experimental success is rewarded with survival. Failure with extinction. The natural world never deludes itself. Only people do that.

No duck or other animal is going to reason its way to an understanding of nuclear physics. But at the same time no duck or other animal is going to persevere with a belief that has been shown to be false. For example, I have taught my dog that if he comes when I call he gets a treat. To the dog there is an evident causal relationship between his coming when called and the delivery of a bit of dried liver. He has tested the hypothesis a thousand times and it has been shown to be true, apart from the rare occasions when I haven't had any dried liver to hand. But these few occasions can be written off as experimental error.

If, however, I were to call him ten times in a row and never once reward him, it would challenge his understanding of the world. Initially he would try hard to reactivate the reward system. He would return faster, sit more eagerly at my feet, maybe jump and scrabble at me in order to get the liver flowing. But if I continued not to reward him he would revise his view of the world without a backward glance. Judging purely on the evidence available, in accordance with the most fundamental principle of science, he'd simply stop coming. Which explains why dogs don't pray.

The whole of evolution is founded on practical, unwitting science. If something works it endures. If it doesn't, it withers. We alone on this planet believe stuff in defiance of evidence. It would seem to be the flipside of our capacity to reason. And we are endlessly encouraged in this folly by the legions of bullshitters.

7

It's simple: vote for me

Mr Gorbachev,' said Ronald Reagan, in front of the Brandenburg Gate in Berlin in 1987. The old performer paused for rhetorical effect and cocked his head slightly to one side in a manner that made him look like a folksy parrot. 'Mr Gorbachev, tear down this wall.'

'Now there's an idea,' thought Mr Gorbachev. And twenty-nine months later, the delay being caused merely by the need to sort out a few administrative details, he tore the wall down.

Which, children, is how brave President Reagan brought freedom, happiness, burgers, iPods, hedge funds, realtors, advertising and all the other joys of capitalist democracy to millions of enslaved people. (And in case you hadn't got the point, he returned to Berlin after the wall had fallen in order to be filmed swinging a sledgehammer against one of the bits left standing.)

It's a story, and for Republicans it's the sort of story they like. Its virtue, as with all effective tales, is its simplicity, but that simplicity is based on a post hoc fallacy. Reagan said what he said and the wall came down. But there is no evidence that the wall came down because Reagan said what he said.

Historians have offered and will continue to offer numerous reasons for the Berlin Wall coming down when it did. What is clear with hindsight is that it was bound to come down. The monstrous, tyrannical edifice of bullshit that the Soviet Union had become under Stalin and his gargoyle successors was doomed eventually to implode. It awaited only the moment when outrage and poverty outweighed fear, and the sole point at issue was not if that would happen but when. You could argue that Reagan's speech brought that date forward a few months. But you could also argue, and perhaps more plausibly, that it delayed it.

Even the reforming Gorbachev would not want to be seen as taking advice from the president of a country that his people had been encouraged to revile.

Politics is a messy business, in the sense that precise cause and effect can rarely be distilled from the chaos of human activity. The wood is vast, the trees innumerable, and discerning any pattern to the forest is beyond most of us. But we want to see patterns. We crave clarity. Which is why the post hoc fallacy is a staple of political bullshit.

Those contending, as I write, for the Republican presidential nomination are keen to pin blame on Obama and the Democrats for America's current economic malaise. That he took office when a global financial crisis was at its height and that President Jesus himself would have struggled to reduce the ill consequences is ignored. The post hoc arguments pour from their mouths. Under Obama, x million hard-working Americans have lost their jobs; under Obama, x million decent American families have lost their homes to foreclosure; and so on. The implicit conclusion is that since these things happened while Obama was in the White House, they happened because he was in the White House.

In recent months the graphs of American prosperity have begun to flick upwards again. Jobs have been created. More cars and houses have been sold. The big corporations have made profits again. It has been entertaining to watch the same Republican candidates wrestling with these unwelcome improvements. By their post hoc reasoning, if Obama was responsible for the bad stuff simply because he was in office when it happened, he must be equally responsible for the good stuff.

Some of Obama's opponents have resorted to a neat rhetorical trick. They have argued that the good things are happening not because of Obama's policies, but despite them. In other words, if he hadn't enacted his policies the good things would have happened sooner. But they are merely compounding their deception. It was dishonest in the first place to exploit the post hoc fallacy. It is doubly dishonest to exploit it selectively.

Human society is too complex for us to grasp in its entirety. If it wasn't, there would be only one political system and only one economic theory and all things would be well. But simplicity appeals to us because, like paradise ducks and other sentient creatures, we evolved to handle the simplest possible equation of cause and effect — if x then y or, as my dog might put it, if sit then liver. The post hoc fallacy appears to offer exactly such an equation, so our leaders, who love to please us, seize on it.

I have in front of me a shiny campaign brochure from the last New Zealand general election. It was issued in the name of Ruth Dyson, the local Labour MP. I know her a little and I admire her. She works hard for others yet doesn't take herself too seriously. A good woman, in other words, and a good MP. But a naughty post hoc-ist.

Page two of the brochure displays a box of six simple graphs. Each purports to illustrate how some aspect of life has deteriorated under the current government: '56,000 more unemployed Kiwis under National', '$40 billion more government debt under National', 'Record deficit of $18 billion under National', etc.

In the light of which I was surprised not to see 'Over 10,000 more earthquakes in Christchurch under National'.

8

May I blame Walt?

In the winter of 2011 an emperor penguin washed up on a beach in New Zealand. It was a long way from where emperor penguins live and it was hungry. So hungry in fact that it ate sand from the beach, which did it no good.

But the bird was rescued, cleaned out and sent to Auckland Zoo to recuperate. It was the sort of story that the media love because it touches an emotional nerve. And sure enough the public took great interest, and the bird acquired the name Happy Feet, after a

Disney-style movie about a penguin. Many thousands of dollars were spent in nursing Happy Feet back to health and its devoted keeper became almost as famous as her charge.

In September the bird was crated up, put on a ship and taken to its natural habitat of the Southern Ocean. A chute was let down from the side of the vessel to allow Happy Feet to slide gratefully back into the world it belonged to. But the penguin didn't want to go. It just stood at the top of the chute and didn't budge. Eventually someone had to shove it. It slid down the chute bottom first, seemingly looking back to the comforts of a safe enclosure and unlimited free fish.

Boffins had glued a GPS transmitter to Happy Feet's back. Initial signals suggested the bird was trying to get back to New Zealand, for which one could hardly blame it. But then nature reasserted itself and the bird headed strongly south. New Zealand breathed a nice warm sigh at the thought of Happy Feet returning to its icy world and finding its worried partner and rearing a chick that perhaps, one day, might make a pilgrimage to the shores of New Zealand and raise its little flipper in grateful salute and— but then the transmissions abruptly stopped. It was possible, said the boffins, that the transmitter had failed. But it was more probable, they acknowledged, that something big had eaten Happy Feet.

It was a delicious moment and not just for the something big. It was delicious for anyone who enjoys it when the orca of reality crunches down on the penguin of bullshit. The specific variety of bullshit here is Disneyfication, a selective and sentimental falsification of the nature of nature.

An emperor penguin is an organism with its place in the food chain. Naming it doesn't alter that fact. One might as well name the orca that ate it, or the fish that the penguin eats or the shrimp that the fish eat. Disneyfication is a form of bullshit that has become increasingly prevalent the more removed we as a species have become from the realities of the planet we inhabit.

Knut was one of two polar bear cubs born in 2006 in Berlin Zoo and then rejected by their mother. Using a net on a stick, zookeepers scooped the cubs off the rock where they'd been left to die and put them in incubators. Knut's brother still died but Knut pulled through to become the symbol of the zoo. The media flocked, visitors flocked, the American ambassador was photographed with him, a million stuffed fluffy toy replicas of his charm were sold, both he and his keeper became globally famous and the value of shares in the zoo doubled. Knut was profitable.

Then in 2010, at the age of four, in front of 600 spectators, Knut trembled, fell backwards into his pool and drowned. The public wept as one and the authorities are now planning to put up a memorial to Knut. What the inscription on the memorial will be I can't tell you but may I suggest 'Disneyfication makes money'. And while I'm at it, may I also suggest two people who won't be laying a wreath on Knut's shrine. They are the parents of an Eton schoolboy who went on a camping trip to the Arctic in August 2011. A polar bear attacked their camp and killed the lad. The bear was shot.

Disneyfication of the world starts young. I was raised on Beatrix Potter books: Jemima Puddleduck, Squirrel Nutkin, Peter Rabbit and other anthropomorphs. I loved them, felt for them in their travails. So much so that when, at the age of perhaps seven, I found a wounded squirrel in the road I immediately went to pick it up. I would nurse it back to health, tame it and train it to sit on my shoulder. The squirrel had other ideas. It sank its teeth into my finger to the bone.

When evil Mr McGregor, the gardener and representative of my own species, captured all Peter Rabbit's nephews and nieces (they'd fallen asleep after eating, as I recall, too much lettuce.

It was where I learned the word soporific) I was appalled by his plan to give them to the unseen but villainous Mrs McGregor, who would bake them into a pie. Fortunately Peter Rabbit managed to extract his relatives from the sack in which they'd been imprisoned and replace them — how, it was never made clear — with shoe brushes, much to the distress of Mr McGregor and the delight of me, the little reader who had been emotionally manipulated to side with the rabbits.

One takes a slightly different view of rabbits in New Zealand. Here they were deliberately introduced by nineteenth-century settlers as a source of wild protein, as pie filling, in other words, for the Mr McGregors who had fled here to escape the feudal servitude of Victorian England. The rabbits took one look at New Zealand's green and pleasant pastures and set about eating it and breeding. Mrs McGregor could have baked pies all day without denting their numbers. Rabbits remain a pest here, so much so that they are now subject to an annual Easter Bunny Shoot, the title of which neatly and simultaneously skewers two widely disparate varieties of bullshit.

I cannot abide cruelty to animals. The word humane is unique to our species and one from which we should take pride. We invented kindness, and the developed world is kinder to the animal kingdom, or at least to some members of it, than it was even fifty years ago. May such progress continue. But at the same time it would be nice if we saw the animal kingdom and our place within it through plain, rather than emotionally distorting, glass.

9

The puppy that never grows up

Because it wilfully misrepresents the actual world we live in, Disneyfication is not only bullshit but it is also a form of child abuse. Parents surround their offspring with fluffy stuffed parodies of top-end predators. It's as if they were trying to swaddle the child in threatlessness, to draw the world's sting. Yet were one of those predators to nudge open the bedroom door and stick its muzzle round the jamb there would be instantaneous panic.

Similarly parents will read the child a bedtime

story of the Three Little Pigs even while the kid is digesting its supper of bacon sandwiches. I once taught a ten-year-old who simply would not believe it when I told her what an egg was and where it came from. She dismissed the notion as gross.

Quite why we Disneyfy the world for kids I don't know. I doubt that hunter-gatherer societies did. I doubt that farming families do. Indeed I suspect it is possible only in cities. But once the sentimental seed has been sown, the crop of commercial gain is readily harvested, not least, oddly enough, by Disney.

Disneyland is a bloodless, synthetic heaven where the lion lies down with the lamb. On arrival you are likely to be greeted by a human being dressed as a mouse. The mouse is fully clothed but lacks any genital bulge. It is capable of only one facial expression, which is a grin. Inside the mouse costume the employee may be a lank-haired misanthrope but externally he is and can only ever be a joyous and loving mouse. Meanwhile, were an actual mouse to be found in the Disneyland kitchens, they'd be on the phone to Rentokil before you could say hypocrisy.

The image of the man in the Mickey Mouse costume will serve as a metaphor for the Disney company itself. It's a corporation. It exists not to promote joy, nor to cheer up sick children, nor to sanitize the world. It exists to make money. Should it cease to do so it would cease to exist. The image of happiness, the denatured nature, the sexless animals, the drenching sentimentality, these are the snake oil that it sells. Behind the perpetual grin is a granite-faced devotion to profit. The company occupies, and adheres to the rules of, a commercial world that is as competitive and ruthless as the natural world it makes its money by misrepresenting. It behaves, in other words, in its self-interest and urge to survive, precisely like a mouse, an actual mouse, a mouse that gnaws its way into the pantry and nibbles at your groceries, a tiny beast that can cause enormous human beings to leap onto a stool and scream.

If I step out of this basement study, I emerge into the garage where there's a dirty Toyota Carib, a few tools and a toilet with a sliding door that sometimes doesn't. The corners of the toilet floor are littered with mosquitoes that die there in vast numbers for reasons I am ignorant of. Above the cistern is a shelf, and on the shelf a 'family' pack of sixteen Kleenex toilet rolls. And beaming from the side of the plastic packaging around these toilet rolls is a puppy. It's a labrador puppy, only a few weeks old, and it appears to be smiling. I don't know whether the good people at Kleenex tweaked the photo a bit, but the dog's lips are noticeably upturned.

I like soft toilet tissue because I remember its predecessor, the shiny and densely interleaved paper that came in a box. It was sturdy but there its virtues ended. It was cold, it produced a crease as sharp as a blade and rather than removing what it was tasked to remove it tended merely to redistribute it. Soft tissue was a vast improvement. But its manufacturers were faced with the problem of how to promote it. Any literal reference to its function or its qualities — 'Collects what other papers leave behind!', 'Your finger won't go through it!' — was unlikely to go down well. Nor were you likely to find a celebrity to endorse the stuff, and thus expose his or her reputation to the inevitable peristaltic jocularity.

Whoever came up with the puppy as a conflationary metaphor for the unmentionable paper was a marketing genius. Like a puppy, the paper is light in colour and soft to the touch. That's about it for legitimate similarities, but they were more than enough to set the conflationary ball rolling. But conflation was not the sole reason for the campaign's success, nor even, I'd suggest, the principal one. (And it has been such a success that it has persisted for over half a century.) What the puppy did was to tap into Disneyesque sentiment.

Many people dislike dogs, but just about everyone

likes puppies, at least on sight. They're so cute, playful and adorable, a sales pitch made flesh. Which is exactly what they evolved to be. Puppies need to appeal to the bitches that whelped them, otherwise they are likely to be neglected.

Bitches are mammals like us. Indeed we and they share such quantities of DNA that we are more similar than we are different. So it is unsurprising that the qualities that render a pup appealing to a bitch also render it appealing to us: those huge eyes, that snub nose, that soft vulnerability. It is precisely these qualities in our own species that cause certain people to lean into a pram and acquaint its occupant with terror.

The maternal urge to love and protect is a powerful and positive emotion that goes beyond words. If by conflation the makers of bog roll can attach a ghost of that urge to their product they are likely to be on to a good thing. But at the same time they are selectively denaturing the natural world.

The point about the Kleenex puppy is that it's a puppy with no downsides. It never shits on the carpet or chews the furniture. More significantly still, it is perpetually a puppy. In fifty years the adorable beastie hasn't got a day older. In the actual world a puppy gets a day older more or less every day. And those days add up fast so that within a few months it becomes a dog. And once that happens its mother stops feeling sentimental about it and shoos it away.

Some people do the same. In the pet shop they fall for the puppy's sales pitch of cuteness. But within the year they find they have something less winsome on their hands, whereupon they shoo it to the vet to have its inconvenient doghood — and you have to admire this euphemism — put to sleep. Thus the dog becomes a blameless victim of the Disneyfied mind.

The nub of Disneyfication is the denial of sapid reality, the sanitization of a blood and sinew world. Its aim in so doing is to foster a sentimental response. Sentiment and reason are not bedfellows. And since reason is the bullshitter's perpetual enemy, arousing sentiment serves the bullshitter well. Indeed the arousal of emotion is the weapon that the bullshitter reaches for most often. Almost any emotion will do. The bullshittee under the influence of any feeling from love to loathing, from disgust to delight, is easier to manipulate. The bullshitter's mantra is 'Just make the buggers feel something'.

It isn't hard. We are emotional creatures and we like it that way. The life of pure reason is unappealing. If we were given the choice between living as Mr Spock or Captain Kirk, we'd go for Kirk. He can think but he can also feel. Not to do so is not to be human. It is our nature. But it is also our vulnerability.

Bullshitters know this. And the irony is that they know it rationally. The bullshitter makes a rational decision to suppress rationality in others. It is hard to sell anything to Mr Spock, or to convince him to vote for you, or wage war for you, or to get him along to sing on a Sunday morning. Kirk is an easier target.

10

It's natural, see

Arthur the beekeeper lent me a mask but he drew the line at gloves. 'You can't work bees with gloves,' he said.

He smoked the hive, prised the lid off and told me to lift out a frame. It was heavy with honey and thick with bees. The whole thing thrummed. A bee settled on my wrist. With my hands holding the frame I tried to blow it off. It stung me. 'I've just been stung,' I said. Arthur laughed and urged me to ignore it. More bees had settled on my wrists and the backs of my hands.

I was tense with fear. Another one stung me. I thrust the frame at Arthur and ran. It was a poor decision. As I ran, swatting wildly, I collected perhaps a couple of dozen stings.

That evening my arms and hands swelled and the flesh hardened. Nausea rose in my throat. I grew hot and sick. I didn't sleep that night. The next morning the doctor gave me something, I forget what, but it was still several days before the stuff was flushed from my system and I came right.

'Bee Venom Mask …', runs an ad for Abeeco, 'has taken the beauty industry by storm with reports of royalty and other well-known celebrities using NZ bee venom.' For $89.95 you can get a 50-gram pottle of the Bee Venom Mask. Or for $38, you can acquire 9 grams of Bee Venom Lip Plumper, for 'beautiful plump, luscious looking lips'.

Now I do not for one moment doubt that bee venom does wonders for the appearance, that it plumps the lips, that it takes years off you and that, as the Abeeco website avers, 'it was credited with making Camilla, 63, look years younger'. After all, it plumped my own skin very nicely. What interests me, however, is that Bee Venom Mask 'has been hailed as Nature's natural alternative' (to Botox apparently). Ignoring the passive verb which fails to reveal who's doing the hailing, and ignoring also the spectacular redundancy of 'Nature's natural', which implies that Nature is just as liable to produce unnatural stuff, I draw your attention to the word Nature.

The capital letter suggests personification. We are invoking that benign goddess, Mother Nature, a sweet old dear who has our interests at heart and who could not be cruel to us. What she does is good, simply by dint of being what she does. If something is natural it implicitly follows that it is beneficial.

Now, the topical application of minute quantities of bee venom may indeed be good for your appearance. But the subcutaneous injection of not much more of the stuff made me as sick as I have been in the last ten years. The stuff was undeniably natural and it was equally undeniably poisonous. So poisonous indeed that if I'd suffered another few dozen stings I might well not have been here to write about it. I'd have been killed, naturally.

Natural is one of the hardest-working words in the bullshitter's lexicon. It has become effectively a synonym for good. It is bullshit because natural does not necessarily mean good. If we define natural as meaning something that occurs without the intervention of humankind, then anthrax is natural, earthquakes are natural, the great white shark that killed an Australian surfer yesterday is natural, and both cold-blooded and warm-blooded murder is profoundly natural. The entire natural ecosystem is founded on organisms murdering other organisms and eating them.

Furthermore, to define natural as meaning all the stuff on earth except people is absurd. Only the wilfully blind deny that we evolved in the same way as everything else. We are as much a part of the fabric of nature as anthrax is, or the great white shark, or the kowhai tree in my garden or the bellbird that sucks the nectar from its flowers. I presume that a bellbird's nest would also be considered natural. If so, then why not a human being's house? And if a house is natural, then the same ought to be true of a skyscraper, a car, an atom bomb, an iPhone, and anything else that human ingenuity has devised in the same way as a bird builds a nest.

But the bullshitter's use of the word denies this. The implied antithesis of natural is artificial, in other words man-made. Thus it suggests, though never quite states, that if we could only return to a state of nature, could rediscover harmony with the natural rhythms, or some sort of similar ill-defined notion, all manner of things would be well. They wouldn't. As Thomas Hobbes observed in three memorable adjectives that have outlived him by 300 years, humankind in a state of nature lived a life that was 'nasty, brutish and short'. What has enabled you and me to live a life that is nicer, more civilized and longer are the discoveries and inventions brought about by the exercise of reason, in other words the artificial stuff, from polio vaccines to a sewerage system. All of which is excluded from the bullshitter's implicit definition of the word natural.

That definition is sentimental. It could only be foisted on a public that has lost sight of the actual world it inhabits, the Darwinian world where only the fittest survive and where 99 per cent of all the species that have ever evolved have become extinct, just as we will.

In short, the term natural as commonly used is without meaning. It is merely a noise, designed to evoke a sentimental response. That response bypasses or numbs the faculty of reason. Natural has become what A.J. Ayer called a hoorah word — no one knows quite what it is but everyone's for it. As a result it gets pinned to a host of things for sale: bed linen with magnets sewn into it, strawberry-flavoured yoghurt, ventilation systems, frozen dog food … The list is endless.

I have in front of me a bottle of moisturizing shower

milk. The puffery on the back announces that the maker 'uses simply the best ingredients from nature to leave your skin clean and noticeably softer'. Here are those ingredients: 'Aqua [how's that for bullshitterish chutzpah?], sodium laureth sulfate, cocamidopropyl betaine, fragrance, sodium chloride, styrene/acrylates copolymer, cocamide MEA, sodium benzoate, sodium salicylate, citric acid, polyquaternium-7, glycol distearate, tetrasodium EDTA, lactose, honey, milk protein, CL 19140, CL 16035.'

And the name of the range to which this shower 'milk' belongs? *Naturals*, of course.

It wasn't always so. Four hundred years ago, Shakespeare had a far more accurate image of the nature of nature. 'Thou, Nature, art my goddess,' announced Edmund in *King Lear*. 'To thy law my services are bound.' Edmund was the bastard, or 'natural', son of the Earl of Gloucester. When he said these lines he was proclaiming that he was going to act like the bastard he was. He would traduce his loyal (and legitimate) brother, deceive his gullible dad and act purely in malicious self-interest. He'd get as much power and wealth for himself as he could. He didn't care whose fingers he stamped on. Pity, sympathy, kindness be damned. This was how nature worked, without compunction and without conscience. And the bastard was bang right.

Contrast this with the song that in 2001 was voted New Zealand's official top song of all time (well, since 1840). It was written by Wayne Mason and it was called 'Nature'. Its refrain is 'Nature, enter me', which is more or less the same request as Edmund made. But between Edmund the bastard and Mason the songster there lies a romantic revolution that began the process of inverting and falsifying our view of the natural world.

Just as Edmund did, Mr Mason personifies nature, but unlike Edmund he considers her (she's always she) to be benign and gentle. 'Up in a tree a bird sings so sweetly' runs one line of the lyrics. These words suggest that the bird is merely voicing the sheer joy of being alive. But this is to misrepresent it. The bird's 'song' serves two purposes. One is to proclaim its territorial rights — a sort of aural 'Trespassers Will Be Prosecuted'. The other is to attract a mate in order to reproduce. (The second of these purposes is also true of pop singers.)

The common contemporary attitude to nature is essentially religious. Lurking behind the word is a suggestion of a mighty yet benign spiritual entity who is on our side. If we do not stray from her ways she will look after us, cure us of our ills, make us happy, love and nurture us. She won't. For evidence spend one night alone in the Amazon jungle without such artificial encumbrances as clothes, tent, gun or light. Nature will enjoy the encounter.

(There is one particular Amazonian beastie that I have long admired and which you might like to keep an eye out for. It's an amphibian that hangs around in the river's backwaters, waiting for a passing mammal to urinate. With a single prodigious expenditure of effort the critter somehow projects itself *up* the stream of urine and, having reached the source, takes hold and starts burrowing. A while later it lays eggs that hatch inside its mammalian host. The darling offspring then exit the way Mother entered, to spend their lives splashing happily about in the Amazon until they are grown up and fertile, whereupon they will lie in wait for the next passing mammal with a full bladder. Nature, enter me indeed.)

As with many religions, the soppy veneration of sweet Mother Nature includes an element of self-hatred. Nature is nice and we bugger it up. The notion is a staple of the tourism industry, which tempts us with juicy images of virgin forests, lakes and beaches, unpeopled, Edenic. And the adjective it reaches for with tedious predictability is unspoilt. These places are as they were meant to be. What a glorious, scenic wonderland the world would be if only we weren't part of it. So hurry now and enjoy one of the few remaining bits of wilderness before it goes.

One obvious irony is that by selling the place to tourists the industry furthers the spoiling. Tourists need hotels, and a sewerage system and nice safe walkways in order to get the authentic wilderness experience. All of these things play their part in changing, or spoiling, that same wilderness. Whereupon the tourism operators find somewhere else that's pretty and start again.

A further irony, of course, is that most people want wilderness only on their terms. They want to photograph it from a distance, dabble a little at its safe edges, and then withdraw to precisely the comforts of civilization they believe they've come there to avoid. Were the place actually and unrelievedly natural they wouldn't like it at all.

There is also a flip side to the soppy veneration of nature. I was reading the ads in a real estatist's window in London Street, Lyttelton. I had my dog on a lead. Also reading the ads was a youngish mother who was holding hands with her daughter aged perhaps six. Unnoticed, the child reached out and patted my dog. His tail wagged and soon there was such a love-fest going on between them that the girl giggled. Mother looked down, yanked the girl away with a ferocity that threatened the child's shoulder joint and said, 'How many times have I told you? Animals are dirty. We're going home to wash right now.' Hauling the child off at speed, the mother nevertheless found the time to turn and give me and my dog a look so filthy I felt in need of a wash myself.

Her actions nicely illustrated not only how to hand on a neurosis to the next generation, but also an inversion of the nature-is-nice delusion, to wit, the belief that nature is unrelievedly hostile. It is a less common form than the soppy version but it is every bit as much a delusion. And it, too, can be put to commercial use.

There's a television programme called *How Clean Is Your House?* or something similar in which white-coated busybodies take swabs from under the sink or behind the toilet and discover, to the horror of the householder, that the place is shoulder deep in germs. Quite why the householder submitted to the intrusion in the first place I have no idea, nor have I watched enough of the programme to discover how it winds up. Perhaps a SWAT team is sent in wearing masks and overalls, armed with spray guns of a disinfectant that will blister paint, and thus saves the householder from death by germs and everyone is happy ever after. Indeed I wouldn't be surprised to learn that the show was sponsored by a maker of such ferocious disinfectant, because they often do something similar with their advertising.

A toddler crawls towards a plastic toy. The camera zooms in on the toy and suddenly it's as if you are looking through a parody microscope — it's science, see — and the surface of the toy is shown to be crawling with, well, with germybuggy sort of things, coloured fluoropurple. The microscope camera tours the room discovering fluorescent germybugs on the lips of the adorable border collie, on the telephone, on the side table, until Mum, svelte, loving and wise, arrives with an improbably clean sponge and a bottle of branded disinfectant and the germybugs disappear with a single stroke of the improbably clean sponge and thus life is made safe for junior.

Or in a different version the camera takes us down into the carpet across which junior is so adorably crawling and discovers down there among the cut pile a Jurassic Park of miniature beasties with nibbling mandibles and far too many legs, all of them eager to latch onto junior's unblemished puppy-fat. Enter Mum once again, defender of the weak, armed this time with a branded vacuum cleaner and the sort of smile we all wear when vacuuming. Up the pipe goes Jurassic Park and with it the threat to junior's wellbeing.

As with the sentimental view of nature, the implicit assumption is that humankind is distinct from the natural world. Only now the natural world is not our friend but our bristling remorseless foe. Were it not for the vigilant forces of hygiene and technology it would soon be gnawing at our lifeless bones. Which is every bit as dishonest, as untrue to how things are, as the syrup of Disneyfication. The natural world on which we are entirely dependent, and of which we are so evidently part, is neither for us nor against us. It is simply indifferent to our welfare.

11

Be afraid

One winter's evening, when I was about seven, I had been playing at Kevin Toohey's house and left my return a bit late. As I set out for home the light was fading and I decided to take the short cut up Orchard Lane. At the near end there were a couple of bungalows and the comfort of a street light. But then the lane kinked and I was in darkness. There were trees to either side. I could hear leaves swishing. I looked over my shoulder.

I did not then know Coleridge's lines:

Like one, that on a lonesome road
Doth walk in fear and dread,
And having once turned round walks on,
And turns no more his head;
Because he knows, a frightful fiend
Doth close behind him tread.

But I doubt that they'd have helped.

I had perhaps 400 yards to go to reach the cutting through to Wilmington Close. I started to run but the sound of my feet merely added to the fear. I think I was whimpering. When I reached home I found I had soiled myself. Abundantly. It was the first and only time since infancy, up till now at any rate. And it was fear that did it.

Thomas Hobbes, he of the nasty, brutish and short, saw fear as one of the two fundamentals of human, and presumably animal, behaviour. The other was desire. Desire impelled you towards things, fear held you back. Every action you performed was the outcome of a tug of war.

Fear is rooted in the most primitive parts of the brain, the pre-linguistic bits, the bits that we share with other mammals and that go back to our evolutionary roots. When my dog is scared the signs are obvious — the flattened ears, the hunched spine, the cringing posture, the tail whipped between the legs like an inverted question mark. The sight evokes pity in me, an urge to console.

The effect of fear on our own bodies is similarly drastic: the shudder, the gulp, the tingling uprush of nausea, the quickened pulse, the widened eyes, the withdrawal of blood from the face so as to concentrate its resources where it matters; these effects are physiological and quite involuntary. The very mechanism of the body is compromised. We become literally different. For as long as fear lasts, which is until its cause is either destroyed or avoided, fear governs what we do. It supersedes everything else, for the very good evolutionary reason that those of our ancestors who were fearful stood a better chance of surviving. Those who weren't tended not to be around long enough to become ancestors.

The most potent fear is of the unknown or unseen. The known or seen can be faced, the consequences dealt with. I would have been grateful in Orchard Lane, for example, if the bogeyman had actually materialized and tried to do whatever it is that bogeymen do. (My thinking, arrested by fear, had not considered the bogeyman's possible intentions. If it had, I might have calmed down a bit.)

But the bogeyman remained in the shadows and

so fear kept its grip and my bowels relaxed theirs. I was gibbering and feeble, desperate for succour, and quite beyond reason, a condition that would cause any purveyor of bullshit to salivate. Which is why the exploitation of fear, and especially fear of the invisible, has been a favourite weapon in the bullshitter's armoury since bullshit began.

About 3 miles from Orchard Lane, near where the London to Brighton railway ducks into a tunnel through the South Downs, stands Clayton Church. It's the standard English parish church, evocative, enduring, endearing. On its walls are murals close to 1000 years old. They depict, among other things, the Last Judgment. They lack the gory inventiveness, and the sadistic delight, of Hieronymus Bosch, but I can remember an image of two hopeless arms flung up in self-defence by a sinner who is being trampled by the hooves of a horse — the medieval equivalent of god running you down in a Humvee. The message is simple: be afraid.

These would have been the only images that Clayton's illiterate peasants saw from one week to the next. The only literate person in the village would have been the priest, the only book the Bible, of course, and it would have been in Latin, a language as remote to the peasantry as Sanskrit. And that was it. That was learning. That was truth. That was how things were.

It suited the church very nicely. The clergy did not have to work. They lived off the work of their 'flock', whom they could tax and over whom they sat in judgment. Understandably the church's one fear, a remote one most of the time, was that the flock might question the authority of the shepherd. The purpose of the murals was to minimize that risk. Keep the people afraid of the consequences of rebellion, or of questioning religious authority, and the job was effectively done. So scare them with hell.

All three successful monotheistic religions use hell to induce fear. This is partly because all three derive from the same source but mainly because it is such a cracking tool of control. Hell resembles the bogeyman in Orchard Lane. You believe it's there, and yet it is always just off stage. Thus it can be neither disproved, nor faced. And it is yoked indivisibly to the instinctive fear of death. At the same time as the church promoted a terror of hell, it also offered a way to allay that terror, which was to obey the church. It was a closed, self-perpetuating and hugely profitable system that remains at work in every theocracy around the globe.

Few churches, however, have ever been content

to leave the punishing to god post mortem. Most have been eager to anticipate his displeasure very much pre mortem. It's almost as though they didn't trust him. The purpose has always been to keep the fear level high and to maintain market share. Hence, for example, the dreadful punishments imposed for heresy or apostasy. It remains the official doctrine of Islam that anyone who renounces the faith be stoned to death.

The best-known fearmongers of history were the Inquisition, a body of doctrinal enforcers first formed in the thirteenth century as a result of a forty-five-year crusade by the Catholic church to stamp out Catharism. The Cathars of south-west France recognized neither the French king nor the Catholic church and they adopted a theology of their own. This the church condemned as the Albigensian heresy. There is dispute about precisely what the heresy comprised, but it seems that the Cathars asserted that all things on earth were the devil's work, that it was therefore impossible to live a life without sin, that god was all loving and would forgive sinners regardless of what they'd done so long as they repented at the last moment, and so really there was nothing to be worried about. Reportedly they lost their fear of hell and became rather licentious.

At that time there was little distinction between the political and the religious. The pope recruited allies and sent in the troops. Those Cathars who would not repent, which was thousands of them, were hanged or burned at the stake.*

A handbook for inquisitors published in 1578 spelled out the importance of inculcating fear: 'for punishment does not take place primarily and per se for the correction and good of the person punished, but for the public good in order that others may become terrified and weaned away from the evils they would commit.'

The ideal time to instil fear is the ideal time to instil everything else: infancy. That's when we're programmed to learn. Hence every church's bid to get in on the ground floor of education, even today. It's sound business practice. I can think of few sayings more sinister than the famous Jesuit observation, 'Give me a child until he is seven, and I will give you the man.' Religious education implicitly admits that god, despite being omniscient, omnipotent and all the fictitious rest of it, needs a helping hand if he is to get into people's heads. It rejoices in repressing the one faculty that has got our species anywhere — the

---

* For a catalogue of the atrocities committed or condoned over the centuries by religious authorities of all brands, I strongly recommend Christopher Hitchens' magisterial polemic *God is Not Great*.

untrammelled, unprejudiced exercise of our limited power of reason.

All the major religions require submission. Islam, indeed, is defined as total submission. Its physical expression is prostration. Five times a day a devout Muslim kneels and then leans forward to touch his face to the ground. That's a lot of self-abasement.

The gesture resembles the kowtow required of anyone entering the presence of the Chinese emperors of old. It was wise to kowtow. The emperor was effectively a god, but a god who was undeniably there and undeniably capable of wrath. The inventiveness of Chinese methods of slow execution for anyone who displeased the emperor was remarkable.

The wrath of god, for very good reason, is never seen. Those things that used to be considered expressions of that wrath — earthquakes, volcanic eruptions and the like — have long been shown to be both explicable by rational enquiry and indiscriminate in whom they choose to destroy. But fortunately there have been plenty of people down the ages who were able to interpret what god might get angry about and who remain happy to take on the responsibility of exacting vengeance on his behalf.

In 2005 a Danish newspaper published a dozen cartoons depicting Mohammed. Nothing much happened. A few Danish Muslims protested and tried to draw the world's attention to what they considered to be blasphemy. One of the few effects this achieved was to cause the cartoons to be republished in over fifty countries. At no stage did Mohammed demonstrate his anger. But four months later thousands of people did. The Danish embassies in Syria, Lebanon and Iran were set on fire. The Danish embassy in Pakistan was bombed. A Pakistani student in Berlin was arrested as he entered the building of *Die Welt* newspaper carrying a large knife. The student admitted his intention to kill the editor. Over 100 people died as a result of worldwide protests.

The people who refused to bow to these threats, who did not prostrate themselves in fear, did a brave thing and a right thing, the thing that has enabled humankind to advance some way from the swamp of superstition and religious tyranny. That roll of honour did not include many leaders of democratic countries whose constitutions are founded on freedom of speech. Their standard diplomatic line was to declare that they were all for freedom of speech, but ... It doesn't matter what followed the but. If you're for freedom of speech, you're for freedom of speech. Any but means you're not.

It also did not include the heads of other churches.

When the mobs and several rabid imams were advocating violence and threatening the lives of civilians, the archbishop of Canterbury and the pope refused to condemn them. They condemned the cartoons. For god's sake.

12

Keep being afraid

On one side of Orchard Lane lay Adastra Park. I spent a large chunk of my childhood there with a mob of other boys, playing endless games of football, cricket and pug. Pug was a hunting game without rules. It took place in the winding sunken stream at the bottom end of the park. There were no teams, though sometimes you would forge, and then break, alliances. The aim was simply to shoot someone.

Your weapon was a whippy stick, to the end of

which you moulded a lump of wet clay. The key to success lay in the clay. Too big or too wet a lump and as you drew back the stick to flick it the lump would disintegrate behind you. Get it right, however, and it was effectively a bullet with a range of perhaps twenty yards. At ten, it could take an eye out. Nanny would have had a fit, of course, but none of us had nannies. Nor did any of us lose an eye.

Our games had a single spectator. I have forgotten his name but he was perhaps fifty years old and famously interested in small boys. He even wore the standard issue flasher raincoat, his hands thrust deep into the, presumably bottomless, pockets. He kept his distance when we played pug because in that anarchic game he was a legitimate target. But when we played football and one team took off their shirts in order to become 'skins' he hovered closer. But he was a nervous man, a jitterer. It was said that he was a former schoolteacher, driven to breakdown by his classes. They used to spike the board-rubber with live match-heads, or so the story went. Anyway, he was timorous and harmless. He merely lurked and watched. Sometimes we'd wave to him.

When we grew a little older, however, and we had more conscious an understanding of his inclinations, we persecuted him. The trick was for one boy to act as bait, peeling off shirt or jeans, while others crept round behind him. Then we'd leap from the bushes roaring. The poor sod would literally jump with terror. He'd stammer, gibber and run, a hopeless old-man run. We'd laugh. I'm not proud of it now.

In one way he'd have a much better time of things today. There would be far fewer mobs of unsupervised boys to scare him. And there would be a greater chance of his stalking a solitary boy and perhaps befriending him. But in another way he'd have it tougher. Adults would be much more likely to trail him, to report him to the police, or even to persecute him themselves. And he might find his name and photo in the papers with the worst of all possible epithets attached. He'd be a paedophile. In Great Britain the word has become so familiar that it is abbreviated to paedo.

I doubt my parents knew the word. I also doubt that there were any more, or any fewer, paedophiles around when I was a kid than today. All that has changed is their profile. And that profile has been changed by the media and politics.

The British Government wants to acquire greater powers to monitor private communications without a warrant. Here is how Home Secretary Theresa May defends the proposed legislation:

Right now, the police and security agencies use information from phone records to solve crime and keep us safe. Looking at who a suspect talks to can lead the police to other criminals. Whole paedophile rings, criminal conspiracies and terrorist plots can then be smashed. Data like this has already helped lock away murderer Ian Huntley. It helped catch the gangland thugs who gunned down Rhys Jones. Last year, police smashed a major international child pornography website based in Lincolnshire. They then used internet data analysis to find other suspected paedophiles. Such data has been used in every security service terrorism investigation and 95 per cent of serious organized crime investigations over the last ten years ... As Home Secretary I have a responsibility to keep the British public safe. That is exactly what I intend to do.

Nice of her, of course, but bullshit. Ms May can no more keep the British public safe than I can win the Olympic 100 metres.

The British public has never been safe. Safe means free from danger and no one is free from danger until he or she is dead. Dangers abound. There is a good chance that while you read this chapter at least one member of the British public will die on British roads. Nor is the British public safe at home. Home bristles with mortal threats: stairs, stoves, light sockets, toasters, stepladders — they all kill. Pyjamas too. Several Brits a year slip both of their legs into one leg of their pyjamas, stand up, fall down, bang their heads and die. The lavatory is more lethal still. Dozens suffer cardiac arrests while straining at stool. Dying peacefully at home, they call it.

But in terms of relative safety, the great British public has never been safer. They live longer than they ever have. Therefore there must be fewer threats to their wellbeing. Yet it is a curious truth of human nature that perceived dangers multiply as actual dangers decrease. The British public is more timorous today in its peace and prosperity than it was in 1940, when it was far poorer and threatened with a brutal invasion. It's as though we are evolutionarily inclined to distrust calm. The less threatened we are, the more we seek threats.

People in power are only too happy to supply those threats. Ms May is ostensibly reassuring the public. Fear not, my little chickadees, she says, I shall fold you all to my capacious breast and guard you from the nasties, from terrorist plots, from criminal conspiracies, from whole (as opposed to partial) paedophile rings (rings?). Actually she is deliberately scaring the public.

Terrorists, paedophiles and criminal conspiracies exist. But relatively speaking they are insignificant. Cars kill more Brits every year than terrorists have managed to kill in the last century. (And the greatest cause of premature deaths in the twentieth century, as it happens, and by a factor of several thousand, was governments waging war. Rationally, if Ms May truly wished to keep the public safe she should do everything possible to diminish rather than bolster the power of the state.)

Ms May is effectively invoking bogeymen. Doing so serves her interest because it is a truth as old as mankind that people in power are there because they like power and are keen to get more of it. A scared public is more likely to grant it.

In New Zealand we have less to fear than probably any people on earth. Our soil is fertile, our society democratic, our cops honest and our weather agreeable. We do have one mildly poisonous native spider but it is a timid creature and easily avoided. Otherwise the threats to our wellbeing are negligible. But fear can still be roused.

Fifteen years ago Winston Peters evoked the threat of an Asian takeover of New Zealand through immigration. Thus he tapped into and fostered xenophobia, our instinctive fear of otherness. The gambit was hateful and divisive. It was also bullshit. Asian immigrants, like most immigrants, tend to work hard to forge a new life. And their children assimilate with ease into the society in which they are born. The process is socially refreshing, as demonstrated by the various immigrant groups that created the United States.

But the bullshit worked. Fear got Peters and a gaggle of ineffective followers into Parliament. Whereupon they did nothing about immigration because it wasn't a problem.

The political exploitation of fear follows the pattern of commercial advertising. It stokes an emotion, creates the perception of a need, then offers a way to gratify that need. So, for example, in the early 1990s the National Party ran television advertisements in which the portrait of some leering ill-shaven thug was erased as if by a rubber. The accompanying slogan was 'Rub out the crim'. The none too subtle implication being that if people voted National then crime would disappear. They did, of course, and it didn't, of course. But the arousal of fear in voters, most of whose lives were quite unaffected by crime, had done the trick.

13

Bad news isn't bad news

Do you remember the stockings? Did you even buy a pair at the airport, perhaps? They were supposed to stop your legs swelling and the veins in them blocking or bursting. The malady was known as deep vein thrombosis, abbreviated from familiarity to DVT, and you were supposed to contract it when you took a long-haul flight. Why going up in the air did this to your legs (though not to your arms) was never made plain. But a decade ago it received considerable coverage and for a while was considered a threat to our wellbeing.

And then, somehow, it disappeared. As far as I know planes didn't change and neither did legs or the veins inside them, but it seemed that one no longer threatened the other. No one to my knowledge announced that the threat had been warded off, or that the medical science, if there ever was any, had been wrong. The idea of DVT just receded like the tide, leaving the strand littered with stockings out of which someone had made money.

At 11.59 p.m. on 31 December 1999 I was walking along Harmans Road with Pete, Lois and three fine dogs. All the dogs are now dead, rest their bones. The night was damp and cloudy. We were going from my place to Pete and Lois's because I'd run out of booze with which to toast the new millennium. But we timed it wrong. The global odometer performed its big tick while we were walking past some insignificant pine trees. (Apt really, because the significance of the moment was spurious. The universe knows as little of our efforts to tame it with a calendar as dogs do. The millennial moment was just another arbitrary point on time's unimaginable continuum.)

Anyway, ships' sirens sounded. Fireworks went off. We could vaguely hear cheers and singing from the crowd in the port far below. But the three of us looked upwards. We half-hoped to see planes spiralling to earth, because their ill-programmed computers were unable to cope with the change of prefix from 19 to 20. No planes came down, of course. Indeed as far as I am aware no computer systems anywhere crashed. Either Y2K had been averted by the hordes of consultants who scurried around fixing things in exchange for great wads of propitiatory cash, or it had been a myth.

I doubt that either Y2K or DVT was deliberately generated to deceive. Most things are never meant. I suspect that each arose as a genuine question, a possibility of a threat that found its way into the media and gained purchase in the collective mind. What they have in common is technology. And what they both latched onto was a latent fear, a suspicion, that we've got above ourselves, that we've been a bit too clever for our own good, and that retribution is due. We've perverted the world and the world will strike back. We've stolen fire from the gods and the gods will strike back. We've subverted the natural order, and the natural order will strike back. We've flown too close to the sun.

This fear seems an ancient one, as the myths alluded to suggest. It is, I think, an expression of perceived, or perhaps merely sensed, vulnerability. The ease of my existence is entirely dependent on technology that I do not understand and cannot replicate or repair. My car's engine is a mystery, my computer even more so. I don't know how to make metal. I couldn't spin cotton into cloth. Though I can read and write, I have less practical skill, less ability to survive in a raw world, than my remote ancestors who hunted and gathered.

This renders me vulnerable and I sense that vulnerability in a wordless bit of the brain, the same bit of the brain that made my ancestors aware that they were dependent on things that lay similarly beyond their understanding and control. If the seasons failed, they starved. So they did what the juju man advised and sacrificed a goat. I just pay the consultant, or buy stockings. But when something comes along to prompt that sense of vulnerability I have to make a conscious decision to judge it on its likely merits rather than to be fearful.

And such a thing comes along with great frequency because the media are keen to bring it to us. The media today are ubiquitous. In our cities it is now hard to escape a screen. They're in our houses, our workplaces and our pockets, in waiting rooms and airports and even in giant form out on the street overlooking our paltry day-to-dayness. And any sort of threat to our wellbeing will make us look at them.

As scare stories, swine flu and bird flu could not have been bettered. The suggestion that a virus had mutated so horrifically that it had crossed 'the species barrier' dug deep into the nervous psyche. No matter that viruses constantly mutate. No matter that plenty of other things cross the species barrier. Here, it seemed, was the natural world taking revenge for us buggering it about. It felt fitting. Here was the plague again, here perhaps was the end of days. As a local virologist put it with regard to bird flu striking this country, 'It's not if, but when.' Though we are still, as it happens, waiting.

The worst thing about these flus, just as with the bogeyman in Orchard Lane, was their refusal to come out of the shadows and put up their dukes. Faced with a horror, people cope. Threatened by a remote horror there is nothing for people to do but feel the preparatory effects of fear.

Also on the bad news principle, the media bring us a constant stream of both geophysical and man-made disasters — a gunman goes berserk in Alabama, a volcano erupts in Indonesia, a tornado sweeps through wherever, floods, fire, suicide bombers and end-of-the-world pestilence. It seems non-stop because it is non-stop. Something is always going wrong somewhere. But the first illusion created by the ubiquitous media is that there are more disasters than there used to be. There aren't. There are just more video cameras. And the second illusion is that they are worse than they are.

In September 2010 the Canterbury region where I live suffered a 7.1 earthquake. It was a bloody good shake and a few buildings fell, but no one died and only one person was badly injured. The cameras descended and reporters from around the globe took it in turns to stand in front of the Westende jewellers in Manchester Street from which the side wall of the upper storey had fallen to expose a domestic interior. It was a strong image. But had the cameras swung through 180 degrees they'd have shown undamaged buildings and people going about their affairs. The world never saw these things.

In February 2011 we got a smaller shake but it was closer to Christchurch and, crucially, shallower. Almost 200 people died and the damage was extensive. A year and a half later we still haven't knocked down all the buildings that need to come down. Once again the media arrived and there was more bad stuff for them to feast on, though it was interesting to note how rapidly we dropped down the bulletins of the international networks. Within a few days there was a catastrophic landslide in South America.

More interesting was how people reacted to the disaster. Almost without exception they coped. There was stuff in front of them to do and they did it. Outsiders praised the resilience of Canterbury people, their stoicism, their good humour, their togetherness. But there was nothing special. All people would react the same way. And there was even an element of pleasure in shared adversity. The difference between the fear of an event and the event itself is vast.

The media need to attract our eyes and ears. Fear serves them well. Their stories are necessarily distortions. The cumulative effect of them is bullshit. Thoreau was on the ball 150 years ago.

If we read of one man robbed, or murdered, or killed by accident, or one house burned, or one vessel wrecked, or one steamboat blown up, or one cow run over on the Western Railroad, or one mad dog killed, or one lot of grasshoppers in the winter — we never need read of another. One is enough. If you are acquainted with the principle, what do you care for a myriad instances and applications? To a philosopher all news, as it is called, is gossip, and they who edit and read it are old women over their tea.

By and large the news you need to know comes to find you. The rest is titillatory.

14

Good old Occam

Bullshit takes two. The bullshitter can pump the stuff out but unless the bullshittee buys it, it seeps harmlessly away. As is plain from preceding chapters, in order to seduce the bullshittee the bullshitter generally plays upon some common quality of human nature. That quality does not have to be a weakness.

For example, one of the chief strengths of the human being is our inventiveness, our ability to imagine and then bring into being things that did not previously exist. It is to this quality we owe tools, bridges, clothes, houses, democracy, everything. But that talent, that urge, to imagine what isn't there can also lead us down the garden path to where the fairies live.

I once gave a speech in aid of a cricketing charity. My reward was to be a guest in a corporate box for a day of test cricket between New Zealand and Australia. Sitting in the window of the box absorbed in the cricket was one of New Zealand's leading businessmen. He's seriously rich, so rich indeed that he now lives mainly in Australia. At lunchtime I was told that this gentleman wanted a word with me.

He was old. I knelt beside his chair, not in homage but to ease conversation. 'Now,' he said, 'you're a clever chap.' (I quote that line merely to show that despite his age he was still very much on the ball.)

I bowed my head and said something suitably modest and dishonest.

'So,' he said, 'what do you make of these crop circles?'

I had heard no recent reports of crop circles. 'Which crop circles?' I said.

'You know, the ones they keep getting in Europe, England especially. What causes them?'

'People,' I said. 'People wearing skis or something

similar to tread the wheat down.'

The old man looked at me with serious surprise. 'You've got to be joking,' he said. 'Have you seen them? Some of them are unbelievably complicated.'

I asked if he thought they were made by aliens. He said, more or less, that there was no other plausible explanation. At that point I turned the conversation round to cricket. But I should have turned it to Occam.

Occam was William of Occam, a medieval Franciscan friar who proposed lex parsimoniae or the law of parsimony, though it isn't actually a law, nor yet a principle of logic. But it's a useful guide in the business of thinking. It proposes that entities should not be multiplied unnecessarily. In other words if something needs explaining and you don't need to create a new entity to explain it, don't.

With crop circles we don't. We have a known entity on hand to solve the mystery. We know that human beings exist near where crop circles appear. We know that human beings can tread on things and are heavy enough to flatten cereals. We know that they are the sole creatures on earth that consciously invent complex and regular patterns. And we even know that they're fond of playing practical jokes. So until we can rule out human agency we have no need to hypothesize aliens. And we especially don't need to hypothesize aliens who cross the universe in vehicles of astonishing sophistication, discover a planet, land on it, and then stay only long enough to do a little decorative damage to a cereal crop before heading home. But irrational aliens, of course, are more exciting than prankster human beings.

The chaplain of a school I taught at could have done with studying Occam. (Actually, all chaplains could. But they would feel obliged in the end to renounce their chaplaincies.) Anyway, on the morning of a big interschool rugby match the chaplain was taking an early stroll round the school grounds, as was his habit. Scattered over the rugby pitch, he found the remains of a freshly killed sheep. Now he hadn't spent years at theological college for no reason. He immediately concluded that some boy or boys had conducted a satanic ritual. Swift were his steps to the headmaster's study and urgent his words.

The head, who in all other respects was an outstanding man, was too indulgent of this chaplain. He listened and he was sufficiently concerned to mention the matter in guarded terms in assembly that morning. If any boy or boys, he said, knew anything of 'untoward events' on the rugby field during the night they were to report to his study immediately after the assembly.

The chaplain had explained the bits of dead sheep by creating a new and unlikely entity — the ritually satanic schoolboy. (Over the course of twenty years' teaching I did meet the odd kid I considered evil but I met no practising satanists.) In the process of leaping to this conclusion he failed to consider whether known entities could have been responsible. Specifically he failed to consider an entity that went by the name of George.

George was a giant mastiff. She (George was short for Georgina) had been whelped on a farm but from puppyhood had shown a propensity for sheep-worrying. She would have been shot had not one of the housemasters resident on campus taken pity on her and brought her to the city where there were no sheep.

Or at least there were ordinarily no sheep. But on the eve of the big rugby match some pupils from the rival school chose to paint a sheep in their school colours and smuggle it onto the rugby field during the hours of darkness. Sadly they performed their prank shortly before George was allowed out for her late night walk. The housemaster had wondered at the time why George had taken longer than usual to come home. Later that night she was sick. And later the following morning he put two and two together and reached the conclusion that perhaps he ought to front up to the head to put things straight.

The *Holmes* show on TVNZ was ostensibly a news magazine programme, but it was also a pioneer in infotainment. One evening in the early 1990s a substantial chunk of the show was devoted to a live studio performance by a visiting British medium.

Before the show the medium asked the studio audience to nominate dead people they'd like to get in touch with. All she wanted to know was whether they sought a father, or sister or daughter or whatever. She didn't explain why, given her paranormal powers, she needed that information, nor, it seems, did anyone ask her. When the medium entered the studio she made it clear that she was being pestered by the fluttering spirits of the dead. 'Not now, sweetheart,' she'd say, flicking her eyes up to the right, 'wait your turn', or some similar guff.

Then, 'I'm getting a young girl,' she said. 'Has anyone lost a young girl?'

And of course someone had. They'd told her in advance.

A hand went up in the audience. The medium would then say something like, 'I see a past trauma and suffering.'

Of course. Daughters rarely die of old age.

The bereaved mother would connive unwittingly in her own deception. 'Yes, yes,' she'd say, 'Emma passed on in a car crash', and thus the medium hooked herself a name and some good hard information, which she could use to further bait the hook.

'Emma wants you to know that the pain's all gone now. She wants you to know she's watching over you.'

By now the mother would be crying. And the medium would move on. 'I'm getting an older man. He's not got a lot of hair. He's wearing glasses [while fluttering about the studio?] and he's, how can I put this nicely, just a little overweight [though fluttering].'

Up goes a hand. Sure enough someone's dad had been bald (most older men are), myopic (ditto) and overweight (ditto).

'He's holding a hand against his chest. Did he suffer from some problem in the chest area, perhaps?'

Well, blow me down, Dad had died of a heart attack. The medium was nothing if not well versed in the statistics of the causes of death.

And so predictably on. She'd use probability to fish for fact. Then she'd adopt the fact as if it had been vouchsafed by the dead themselves. If she hooked nothing, it didn't matter. She could just turn to another of the spirits clamouring to say their bit. In other words, just another fraudulent parasite making money out of emotional vulnerability and wishfulness. Nothing remarkable there.

I taped the show and used it often in the classroom. (I've just thought that I should have invited the school chaplain, he of the satanic ritual, to watch the tape. If he hadn't seen through her — and I'm not confident that he would have done — I suspect he'd have accused her of dabbling dangerously in the occult. It's how the clergy invariably describe poachers on their territory. Belief is a competitive business. You seek a monopoly.)

Few boys give much thought to metaphysical stuff. The physical is more than enough to keep them entertained. But when I showed the tape they were invariably impressed. Even the clever ones readily accepted the invitation to imagine something that wasn't there rather than to scrutinize what clearly was there. They believed the woman was talking to dead people. But it took only a few questions to switch on the boys' critical faculties. And once they'd got the idea, they enjoyed seeing through her even more than they'd enjoyed being taken in by her. In about five minutes they shifted from medieval credulity to twenty-first-century scepticism.

But they had to be prompted to do so. They had all the tools of rational thought, but even though they had no skin in the game, and even though they were emotionally unattached, their default setting was belief, and a willingness, when prompted, to invent an unnecessary entity.

People do the same with coincidence. 'I was in the supermarket and I reached for a packet of cornflakes just as someone else reached for it. We looked at each other and who should it be but Joan from next door. Would you credit it? It was spooky.' Yes, I would credit the coincidence. What I wouldn't credit is the spook.

The brain has a habit of seeing patterns. It's one of our evolutionary advantages. It is indispensable to deduction. But its flipside is to see patterns where no patterns are, and to conclude that forces are at work that are not at work. The brain does not register absence of coincidence. On the numerous occasions that the speaker bought cornflakes never once did she remark on her neighbour's absence. The only spook she needs to invoke already exists and goes by the name of statistical probability. What would actually be spooky is if there were never coincidences.

Were our species ever to adopt Occam's simple principle we would be a lot better off and legions of bullshitters would be on the dole.

15

Just give them a tune

Music is emotionally potent. Remove the musical soundtrack from a horror movie and whoa, it's a comedy. Mute the ads on telly and they become absurd. Silence the organ and the wedding feels hollow. Puncture the bagpipes and the Scots lose the battle.

Language struggles to compete with music. Words are our primary tools of reasoning, our means of getting some sort of grasp on the world, but yoke them to music and they become little more than corroboration of the tune. Music bangs a tap straight into the barrel of emotion. By doing so it sedates our critical linguistic faculties. At the opera, only the tunes matter.

The Philippines is a tough place. Its three most popular national pastimes are boxing, cock-fighting and karaoke. The most lethal of these, by some distance, is karaoke. In the hot little bars where they drink Tanduay rum and eat lechon baboy and sing with a gusto that is unstoppably infectious, several people a year are shot dead. One song in particular is the cause of those deaths, a French tune made famous by Frank Sinatra. People get murdered for murdering 'My Way'.

It's only a popular song, of course, and a popular song is not a PhD thesis. But imagine you're having a quiet drink in a pub, perhaps reading the paper or merely staring into nowhere as you allow a glass of something to put out the little fires of dissatisfaction. An old man shambles in. He's clearly on the point of croaking. You try not to catch his eye, but he addresses you all the same.

'And now,' he begins, 'the end is near, and so I face the final curtain.'

At this point, despite the self-dramatising and the pomposity, you'd cut him some slack. It's morally right to show patience and sympathy to a fellow in his final days, even if he is foisting himself on you uninvited.

But then he carries on with the lyrics exactly as per the song. He boasts that he's travelled 'each and every highway'. His regrets are 'too few to mention' but he mentions them anyway. He did what he had to do but he was never one who kneels. When he bit off more than he could chew he somehow managed to both eat it up and spit it out. And so famously on.

Now, at what point would you decide that he was a boaster and a bore? And at what point would you, depending on your nature, either (a) finish your drink, make an excuse and leave, or (b) tell him exactly what you think of his vain, smug, tedious, self-deluding self-promotion?

Put the monologue to music, however, and you have a song known throughout the world, a maker of millions for its author and its performer, and a song that some Filipinos feel so strongly about that they have committed murder in its defence. The reasons are two, I suspect. One is the tune. It's stirring stuff; it puffs the chest. The second is the emotion that it deliberately fosters, a fantasy of indomitability, the heroic ego, bloody but upstanding, defying misfortune, the self as Achilles, a fearless doer of deeds. It's an appealing notion. It's also self-flattering bullshit. The only way you can get away with it is by putting it to music.

Compare 'My Way' to Philip Larkin's 'A Study of Reading Habits'. Larkin's adolescent narrator identifies with comic book heroes, confident he can 'deal out the old right hook' to flatten his evil enemies. But as he ages the fantasy fades and by the final verse, 'the dude who lets the girl down' before the hero appears, or the coward who keeps the store, 'seem far too familiar'. There's truth there. There's self-knowledge. There's none of either in 'My Way'. But 'A Study of Reading Habits' hasn't made millions for Larkin. And no one's been shot for reading it badly.

Music is everywhere: in lifts and the foyers of hotels, in shopping malls and waiting rooms, on telephone answering services and in airports. It provides a sort of amniotic wash, an aural bath of supposedly soothing emotion. It's hard to escape. And a lot of people clearly don't want to. They isolate themselves from the world with iPods.

So ubiquitous is music and so potent that it acts as a prompter of memory, a marker stuck in the continuum of time. Hear an old pop song and even though you may not be able to name it or recall the lyrics, it will take you back. 'A Whiter Shade of Pale' by Procul Harum, for example, takes me to a tent in the Dordogne and a standard case of adolescent unrequited love.

Though the tune is seared into my skull I never learned the lyrics so I've just looked them up and discovered they are quite without meaning. Though the first stanza, for example, is stuffed with literary allusions, uses a vocabulary everyone can understand and boasts conjunctions that imply coherence of thought (if, then, likewise, so), it is incoherent. It is just sonorous noise, like Edith Sitwell on acid, a sort of pseudo-profundity. That doesn't make it a bad song. It illustrates only the power of music to put thought to sleep.

Pop songs are emotional ephemera, stressing the transitory inflamed emotions of youth, of which by far the most musically celebrated is the urge to disseminate genetic material, an urge that goes by the name of love. Put the lyrics down on paper without the shelter of a tune and most are starveling things, which shrivel to nothing under the faintest critical gaze.

Run through the frequencies on the radio, however, and you will see that perhaps 90 per cent of commercial stations are devoted to them. They are there to bathe us in soft feelings, to cheer us up, to keep us going, to prolong our adolescence, and to present us, washed, pink and emotionally vulnerable, to the advertiser. For the purpose of a commercial radio station, as of any commercial enterprise, is to make money. And the station's only source of money is advertising.

A kid I once taught went on to become a DJ for a commercial station. He developed, as they all do, an upbeat style of delivery. However gloomy he might feel, at the microphone he was always Mr Happy from Happytown, and he became successful.

He was on air when the planes flew into the World Trade Centre. He watched the events on a television in the studio and he could barely bring himself to broadcast. The music still played, the ads still ran, but he said that the whole edifice from which he made his living was exposed for what it was, a veneer of synthetic delusion. He's not a DJ any more.

16

O sing of His grace

I attended a state school, but it was modelled on the traditional private school. It was for boys only. We were divided into houses, even though we went home each night. Everyone studied Latin for the first couple of years at least, there was a boisterously sentimental school song, we faffed around in uniform on Friday afternoons doing paramilitary stuff, and though there was no chapel and no chaplain, there was token Anglicanism in the weekly school assembly, consisting of a prayer, a reading and a hymn. At the conclusion of which the Jews and Catholics were allowed in for the holy recitation of the sports results. (They had to stand.)

I've forgotten the sports results, though they mattered at the time, but I can remember quite a few of the hymns, which didn't. No one paid the least attention to the lyrics, of course, which was as well because they constituted an intellectual insult.

'All things bright and beautiful' was not the worst of them, but it will do to illustrate a few of the notions that the church tries to inveigle into young minds by putting words to music. 'All things bright and beautiful', we sang, or murmured, or simply stood through in silence.

All creatures great and small,
All things wise and wonderful,
The Lord God made them all.

We're back at Disneyfication. Nature consists only of nice animals, the bright, the beautiful, the wonderful and the wise (owls, I presume). 'Each little flower that opens', but not deadly nightshade; 'each little bird that sings', but no mention of vultures. And god made them.

A god who's responsible for the good stuff but

not the bad is a staple of religious propaganda, and a remarkably durable one. When Gaddafi was killed we saw film of Libyans firing bullets into the air and shouting, 'Allahu Akbar', god is great. Fine, but what was the great god up to in the preceding decades as Gaddafi's thugs hauled dissidents into his torture houses where the walls were too thick for the screams to escape? Did god condone this? If so he's not good. Or was he powerless to stop it? If so he's not great.

You can see the same thing on the rugby fields of New Zealand. Quite a few professional rugby players are Christian, many of them Polynesian. Some wear a wrist band with a cross on it. Often when a player scores a try he will kiss the wristband and raise his eyes to the heavens in thanks. God got him over the line. But not once have I seen a player knock the ball on or miss a tackle or concede a vital penalty and then kiss his wrist and look at the sky, whether in gratitude or puzzlement or anger. The player's failures, it seems, are his own doing. His successes, god's. God, to change the sporting image, is on a very good wicket.

After the Christchurch earthquake of February 2011, a Canadian woman was interviewed on television. She had been touring the cathedral when the quake happened. Stone fell around her and she was lucky to get out alive. She was understandably upset. But what she deduced from her survival was that 'someone was looking after me'. I can think of better ways of looking after people than visiting an earthquake on them. It's as if someone were to set fire to your house and then expect to be thanked for rescuing you. I also wonder why god chose to look after this woman but let more than 180 others die.

But let's keep singing in the hall of Brighton Hove and Sussex Grammar School circa 1969.

He gave us eyes to see them,
And lips that we might tell,
How great is God Almighty,
Who hath made all things well.

God has not made all things well. This week I learned by email that a former employer of mine whom I'll call Peter, a wise, tolerant, gentle and generous man whom I admire beyond words and to whom I owe a great deal, has been diagnosed with cancer.

According to this versified propaganda, the reason Peter was endowed with lips was not for him to speak kindly and wisely to people, which he does, nor yet to encourage people when they feel weak, which he does, nor yet to provoke thought in them, which he does, nor even to give voice to the thoughts that brew in his own curious inquisitive mind. It was to praise the lord 'who hath made all things well'. All things, by definition, includes cancer.

And if any apologist for the said lord wants to suggest to me right now that Peter's premature illness is part of some mysterious divine plan that it is not for us to question, then I shall bite my own lip and walk swiftly away for fear that I might otherwise swing a fist.

'All things bright and beautiful' consists entirely of assertions, assertions that don't so much lack supporting evidence as contradict every scrap of evidence that exists. But the sentiments expressed are more than wilful, Pollyannaish, self-delusion. They constitute an adult attempt to brainwash children, though admittedly a feeble one that failed.

The hymn was written in the nineteenth century at the height of the Empire, when Britain was growing rich on the exploitation of subjugated peoples in distant lands. If the natives ever got uppity, in went the navy, invariably with god's reps on board to urge them on. The English upper-middle classes had never had it so good. And they were keen to keep it that way. Here's the sixth verse.

The rich man in his castle,
The poor man at his gate,
God made them, high or lowly,
And ordered their estate.

It's simply a gung-ho plug for the class structure, for the social status quo. If god had made people rich or poor it was clearly sinful to try to change things.

Had we been given these lyrics to read in English, ideally with Jack Smithies, the best of all teachers, we'd have shredded them in seconds. Just as we would have had fun in a meteorology class with this verse from 'O Worship the King' (which has a cracking tune).

O tell of His might,
O sing of His grace!
Whose robe is the light,
Whose canopy space.
His chariots of wrath
The deep thunderclouds form,
And dark is His path
On the wings of the storm.

I got an excellent education. It was founded on the exercise of human reason, the faculty that has lifted us out of the swamp, doubled our life span, brought us countless boons, discovered what actually causes thunderclouds, and may even, one hopes, cure Peter's cancer. The weekly hymn was an attempt to numb that faculty through music. While the education we received was implicitly based on the idea that independent thought made things better, the aim of the hymn was to draw us into a flock, unthinking, uncritical, dependent, meek, obedient and cringing.

I have just discovered that the author of 'O Worship the King' was Robert Grant, a devout Scottish lawyer and politician who became Governor of Bombay in the early nineteenth century. I bet Bombay was thrilled. Grant's father, similarly devout, had been prominent in the British East India Company when, as now, there was a problem with China. The British were buying vast quantities of tea, silk and porcelain from China, but were selling the Chinese nothing. The imbalance of trade was ruinous.

The British East India Company's solution to this problem was to establish a monopoly on Indian opium and then to smuggle the stuff into China. They did so in defiance of Chinese wishes, Chinese law and any sense of fair play. The company, which maintained its own private army and which was led by the devout, knew exactly what it was doing. It sought to balance its books by making drug addicts of vast numbers of Chinese people. When the Chinese objected, in went the gunboats.

The lust for power and money is a commonplace of human life. Any study of the history of our species cannot avoid the conclusion that religious faith has made little, if any, difference. Indeed the distinction between religious authority and political authority and military authority has been effectively nil. All forms of authority want a populace that is both cowed and servile. The commonest way of going about getting it is to establish an authority figure so potent that he is venerated and that the thought of challenging his authority is effectively unthinkable.

The simultaneous political and religious uses of music to placate and indoctrinate the mob come together most obviously in national anthems. The dirge that is the New Zealand anthem, for example, begins by invoking the 'God of nations'. I have never heard anyone question the image. Here's a god, and presumably a Christian one, concerned with the petty groupings that his wayward children establish. The song then entreats this god to 'hear our voices'. Well now, if he can't hear our voices, then there is no point in using our voices to ask him to. And if he *can* hear our voices, there is also no point in asking him to.

The song then urges him to take sides and defend our free land. How is not made clear. He is specifically instructed to 'guard Pacific's triple star', though I have yet to meet anyone who can tell me what this is. (And just in case he can't hear us, or prefers, after weighing things up, to defend someone else's triple star, we maintain an army, navy and air force. We thus demonstrate the same distrust in divine power as the far more faithful United States, who are constantly urging god to 'bless America' but who maintain a colossal military arsenal in case he forgets.)

In short the official anthem of our modern, multi-ethnic, democratic state is an incoherent anachronism, illustrating once again that the use of music permits an astonishing quantity of bullshit to pass unchallenged by the etherized intellect.

17

We won

If no one told you your nationality you'd take a while to find you had one. Observation tells us we're part of a family and that we live in a village or town. But the idea of being part of a nation seems remote and artificial. And rightly so. Most national boundaries are arbitrary things established by war. Indeed it is only in war that most countries have ever expressed themselves as entities, the only time that they have come together as a one. Until, that is, we got international sport.

In 2006 England played Portugal in the quarter-final of the Football World Cup. I was on holiday in England and watched the game in a Birmingham living room. The game was decided by penalties. Mark, my host, a successful businessman, father of four and a friend of forty years' standing, couldn't watch. He laughed at himself for it, but he couldn't watch.

England maintained a fine tradition and lost. After the game I went out into the street to smoke. Birmingham had gone quiet. There was little traffic. No kids were playing in the park across the road. There was, it seemed, a national hush, as the people of England absorbed the catastrophe. Then the silence was broken by a thunderous boom. Just round the corner from Mark's house stood a bus shelter, one end of which was a frame for advertising, eight foot tall and made of shatter-proof glass. Someone had shattered it. That force required to shatter it bespoke an extraordinary depth of feeling. And extraordinary depth of feeling acts on the bullshitter as the smell of possum acts on my dog.

When the Moscow Dynamos toured Britain in 1945, George Orwell wrote, 'Sport is an unfailing cause of ill-will ... There cannot be much doubt that the whole thing is bound up with the rise of nationalism — that is, with the lunatic modern habit of identifying oneself with larger power units and seeing everything in terms of competitive prestige.'

It is only with reluctance that I quibble with Orwell, but nationalism isn't modern. It may be lunatic but it's merely tribalism on a grand scale and tribalism has been a stamp of our species, as of other primates, since we evolved. It's primitive stuff, buried deep in an early and wordless bit of the brain. Which is why it appeals to the bullshitter. It is virtually immune to the assault of reason.

The modern Olympics are supposed to promote the fraternity of nations through friendly competition. Whether they do or not is uncertain. There are still plenty of wars. What is certain is that they prompt the same tribal feelings as war does. Hitler famously used the 1936 Olympics both to promote Germany in the eyes of the watching world and to foster nationalism in the hearts of the watching Germans. Plenty of bullshitters have followed his lead. Their reasoning is simple. Medals make citizens proud of their country. Proud citizens are more likely to love their leaders and to fight on their behalf if needed. And they are far less likely to rebel. The only tricky bit is winning the medals.

The totalitarian regimes of the Soviet Union and

East Germany solved the problem in two ways. Having identified potential champions when they were young, they pumped money into their training, and drugs into their bodies. Such drugs indeed that during the 1960s and 1970s the Olympics became a freak show. Two Russian sisters from that time remain seared on the retina of memory: Tamara and Irina Press. They put the shot and biffed the discus and ran the sprints and did the hurdles, did the hurdles so thoroughly indeed that peasants followed for the kindling. The Press sisters collected swags of medals and were paraded as national heroes. It was only when the international athletic authorities decided to introduce sex testing that the sisters simultaneously decided they'd had enough of running and throwing for their country and retired to the Ukraine to care for their ailing mother.

(I remember that while the Press sisters were being lauded from Moscow to Vladivostok I was doing my best, as an eleven-year-old, to feel proud of a forty-two-year-old veterinarian who had won gold for Great Britain in the clay-pigeon shooting. I did not succeed.)

What the Soviets were engaged in was flagrant state-sponsored cheating for the purposes of bolstering a corrupt regime. Everybody knew it. And the Western democracies were so appalled, so outraged, that they followed suit.

When the Olympics became professional, private enterprise proved every bit as good as communist states at brewing drugs to make athletes bigger, stronger and faster, and Western athletes, being as eager as governments for glory, proved even keener to swallow them. Meanwhile governments use taxpayer money to create athletic scholarships and sports academies, as if these weren't inherently oxymoronic. The pay-off for the taxpayer is in medals and national pride. There is no pretence that this is not so. In New Zealand the funding of various sports is explicitly tied to the medals they win. They more they get, the more they get.

The result is a close correlation between the wealth of a nation and its success at the Olympics. And it just so happens that there is a similarly close correlation between the wealth of a nation and the obesity of its citizens. Thus we have the bizarre situation that the fattest nation on earth routinely wins the most prizes for athletic excellence.

(I have long maintained that there should be two sets of Olympic Games. One would have no drug-testing. If athletes chose to do themselves long-term harm in exchange for short-term glory, so be it. I'd enjoy the spectacle. The other Olympics would involve citizens selected at random from each country's electoral roll. Because they would be selected at the last minute, they would have no time to train. You or I could suddenly find ourselves required to take part in the Olympic pole vault. It would be a true test of a country's state of athletic health, and as Mrs Rasmussen of Taumarunui struggled round the track in the 5000 metres it would make compelling viewing. I'm not sure who'd win this competition (Kenya might be a good bet, though it would struggle in the pool) but I am confident that the States would come last. There might even be deaths on the track. (Think of the ratings.)

At the most recent Olympics the women's shot put was won by a New Zealander, Valerie Adams. When she won, the sports commentators and the news-readers and the politicians reached for the first person plural. We had won gold, they said gleefully. No we hadn't. Valerie Adams had. The we is ra-ra bullshit. The only thing that the newsreaders, the politicians, the commentators, Ms Adams and I have in common is that we inhabit the same bunch of windy rocks in the South Pacific. I am justified in taking credit for her triumph to precisely the same extent as I am in taking blame for the crimes of the local rapist.

It is a commonplace to compare international sport with war and it is a legitimate one. The very language of sport, the weary clichés of the commentators, are drenched in militarism: the field of battle, defence and attack, assaulting the line, besieging the goal, throwing everything at them, cutting them down, a barrage of bouncers, potent weapon, shots on target.

Whenever the Romans won a war they would stage a victory parade in Rome, with the returning heroes fêted and wagonloads of booty being wheeled through the streets to delight the citizens. We do the same with sports teams. Elevated high above the mob whose name they bear, they ride the open-topped bus, bruised from the fight, grinning from the victory, waving to the crowd and taking it in turns to hoist above their heads the silverware they've plucked from the grasp of the foreigner, the enemy. Prime ministers invite these heroes to dinner. The country, which has done nothing but sit on a sofa swigging the official beer, is united in self-adulation.

The line between sport and war is a smudged one. For just as sport is a metaphor for war, it can also work the other way round. Last year US intelligence finally tracked down Osama bin Laden. It turned out that, rather than roughing it in the remote mountains of Afghanistan, he'd spent the last few years mooching quietly with his wives in a detached house in suburban Pakistan. It was a tad embarrassing for both sides, really. But anyway, in went a chopperload of Navy Seals. They stormed the house and killed bin Laden.

When the news emerged there were spontaneous demonstrations of joy on the streets of American cities. Groups of young men jumped up and down chanting 'USA, USA'. The triumphalism was indistinguishable from a crowd at Wembley chanting 'Engerland, Engerland'. This parallel was further underlined when the Fox News Channel marked the assassination by selling celebratory T-shirts. The slogan across the chest said, 'Navy Seals 1, bin Laden 0'. (Though bin Laden might reasonably have argued that he'd actually won the game by several thousand goals.)

18

Parochial milking

In *Big Babies: Or, Why Can't We Just Grow Up?*, Michael Bywater argues that modern Western society infantilizes its citizens. Kept in a state of childish emotional dependence, those citizens can be controlled and milked for cash. It's a persuasive thesis, confirmed by the growth of sport as business.

To Shakespeare, sport meant extramarital sex, or learning the skills of war, or hunting animals, or torturing animals. But it didn't mean sport as we know it. Sport as we know it barely existed in the sixteenth century, but Shakespeare's word for it was games. Games were kids' stuff. The people who took part in games were just playing.

Playing games is as instinctive to children as it is to puppies. Games mimic the world they will grow into and foster the skills they will need. Boys and puppies like to play competitive games. They fight for supremacy without drawing blood. Trying to repress this urge is futile, as those who have tried to expunge competition from primary school sport have found. The kids always know who's won.

It is as instinctive for tribes to wage war as it is for kids to fight. So it's a good civilized thing for tribes to wage their wars bloodlessly on the sports field. It acknowledges a destructive instinct and channels it into something athletic and joyous. Over the fifty-something years I've been alive, sport has furnished me with more enduring friendships than any other activity and more pleasure than anything except perhaps literature. Sport is wonderful. And local rivalry adds spice. Each town puts up its local heroes and others turn out to cheer them on. So when the centre forward for, say, Rotherham, bangs one into the net, his neighbour in the stand can exclaim with some pride, 'Aye, that's our Fred.' And the next time he sees him in the pub he can buy him a drink. It's clan feeling, local tribalism, instinctive and understandable. And for these precise reasons it is exploitable. It has been duly exploited.

The Rotherhamite enjoys feeling parochial. But he enjoys even more feeling parochial and victorious. And if the price of victory is to import a player or two, it's a price he is happy to pay. It means that the power unit he belongs to is more powerful and he gets more pleasurable feelings of superiority by association. His allegiance to his feelings proves stronger than his allegiance to authenticity.

So Rotherham buys players from elsewhere. To pay for them it charges people to watch them. And if the team wins, more spectators come, paying money to buy more players and suddenly the team called Rotherham has become a business. In the process there has been a semantic shift. The word Rotherham now means two things: the business and the town. The business exploits the parochial feelings that the name of the town evokes but it has lost all actual connection with that town. In the context of the business, the word Rotherham has become a mere noise, an evocative tool. It has become a brand. And thus the gates are opened to bullshit.

Bullshit rapidly discovered that tribal allegiance is easily aroused and quite amoral. People are happy to associate themselves with anything successful. It does not depend on actual tribal affiliation. It depends only on feeling good. So successful sports teams develop huge followings regardless of their ostensible home. Huge followings make money. Money buys the best players. And so the cabbage swells.

In the 1990s a Russian billionaire bought Chelsea Football Club. He imported a Portuguese manager, and a squad of fine players. None of them came from Chelsea. Few of them could have found Chelsea on a map. But they became a team called Chelsea and they were good and the people flocked and the money followed. Chelsea does not mean Chelsea, any more than Manchester United means Manchester. You can buy shares in Manchester United on the Singapore Stock Exchange. Bangkok hosts a Manchester United fan club.

Sport is simply a business. It sells the thrill of partisanship rather than, say, toilet tissue, but the principle is identical. (Though I would not be surprised to learn that in the Manchester United shop you can buy, along with the Manchester United home strip and the Manchester United away strip and the mugs and the scarves and the signed photos, Manchester United branded toilet tissue. Or perhaps, and this on reflection might sell better, Manchester

City branded toilet tissue. Manchester City, by the way, is not listed on the Singapore Stock exchange. It belongs to an investment arm of the government of Abu Dhabi.)

There seems no limit to the proliferation of sporting businesses. Factitious competitions spring up from nothing. In the 1990s the astute and remorseless Rupert Murdoch, who also, as it happens, owns the Fox News Channel, created a rugby union competition for the benefit of his media empire. The teams were known, indicatively, as franchises.

The franchise representing the region where I live was given the name of the Canterbury Crusaders, ostensibly a nod to Christchurch's Anglican foundation. But it was neatly ironic that a team created by a ruthless acquisitor should be named after a bunch of ruthless acquisitors. And just as medieval kings and popes stirred up religious and patriotic fervour for their own acquisitive ends, so Murdoch has used parochialism to do the same thing. As he clearly understands, it isn't the thing itself that matters — the sport, the religion — it's the feelings associated with the thing. Arouse emotion, inflame it, then exploit it. It's every bullshitter's unspoken mantra, from the pope to the PR whore.

Murdoch's competition boomed. People proved

only too willing to become fans, even while knowing that the competition was synthetic. Cars in these parts are festooned with bumper stickers saying 'Don't cross the Crusaders'. Another nice ironic pun, of course, but one that makes the driver, though he may be a coward and a slob, feel both tough and perhaps clever by association.

Here's a piece of commentary that could have come from the recent Rugby World Cup: 'Arlidge to Thompson … Thompson cuts inside, breaks the tackle, slips the ball to Leitch … Leitch for the line, held up, but oh, a brilliant offload to Nicholas and it's a try, a stunning try.'

To which country would that try have been credited? The answer is Japan. Countries, like commercial clubs, now acquire players from anywhere they can within the increasingly flexible rules. And players, naturally, will go wherever they can get international glory and the money that goes with it. Three of the best four batsmen in the England cricket team were raised in South Africa. African runners compete at the Olympics in the colours of Middle Eastern states that are flush with oil money. Kiwis play for or coach just about every team in the Rugby World Cup. International sport is as much a business as the club version. New Zealand Rugby has a CEO. And when the All Blacks were knocked out of the 2007 World Cup he said, 'The brand has taken a bit of a dent.'

What the twentieth century did was to shift sport from something that people do to something that people watch other people do. The reward for the watchers is emotion by proxy. Whenever one game ends, another looms. Fans are drawn ever forward to the next emotional climax, like herds being led to the shed every morning and evening, world without end, to be milked.

19

The uniqueness of Wayne

Fan is short for fanatic and a fanatic is a religious zealot. The word derives from the Latin *fanum*, meaning temple.

Temples have been built by every human society. They are places where people gather to worship something greater than themselves. Rituals take place, often including prayer, rhythmical chanting, singing and so on. Those attending experience a sense of uplift and of unity, or so I'm told. Temples fall in and out of use. In many parts of Europe the official temples are temples no longer. For most visitors they're now little more than historical theme parks with gift shops. Today's temples, where people still go to find meaning and purpose through ritual, are, most commonly, sports stadiums.

Fans like to be part of a crowd. A sparsely populated stadium is no good because the people remain detached and individual. Only when crammed together can they lose themselves to a mass identity and become that joyously anarchic thing, a mob — a mob with no sense of autonomous dignity, a mob that performs Mexican waves, a mob that even in self-conscious England is willing to sing. 'One Wayne Rooney,' sing the fans of Manchester United, to the tune, I've just realized, of 'Guantanamera', 'there's only one Wayne Rooney.' Which is precisely the sentiment that we sang in school assembly. Only we were extolling god.

At first glance the comparison between god and Rooney seems a good one. Both are male and famously short-tempered. But only Rooney has had a hair transplant. And also, crucially, there actually is only one Wayne Rooney. There are thousands of gods. (As someone else has observed, an atheist disbelieves in all gods. The faithful disbelieve in all gods except one. The difference is mathematically insignificant.)

The best-known choir in English football is the Kop at Anfield, their anthem, 'You'll Never Walk Alone'.

Walk on, walk on,
With hope in your heart …

It's a fine tune and when I hear 20,000 Scousers bashing it out without restraint, something blind stirs within me and I almost want to join them in their abandon, just as I almost do when I hear black gospel singers bashing it out without restraint in some barn of a church in South Carolina.

The sentiment expressed in 'You'll Never Walk Alone' would fit nicely into *Hymns Ancient and Modern*. It is hard to distinguish from:

Yea, though I walk in death's dark vale,
Yet will I fear no ill
For thou art with me; and thy rod
And staff my comfort still.

The most famous manager of Liverpool Football Club was Bill Shankly, a gruff Scot. In my dictionary of quotations he immediately follows Shakespeare. 'Some people think football is a matter of life and death,' said Bill. 'I can assure them it is much more serious than that.' He is half-joking, but only half. Look around a stadium during a tense match and you will see people undergoing emotional extremes. You will see them assume attitudes of prayer. You will see them sway and sing. You will see them enthralled by ritual drama, one that they attend every weekend, something that they look forward to, something that matters to them right then more than anything else, that gives them hope and purpose and that makes them fully alive. Bill Shankly knew exactly what football was doing. It was tapping into what every faith taps into. But unlike any pope or ayatollah, Shankly could be funny about it. He was capable of irony, the saving grace of our species. He acknowledged it was a game.

They know what they're doing at Manchester United as well. As the players emerge from the basement vestry into the temple at the start of the game, the congregation banked on all sides and focused on them and them alone, the players pass under an arch. Above the arch is written the legend 'Theatre of Dreams'. It's bang right. For the ninety minutes to come, roughly the length of a standard religious service, the dream world is established. It is spectacle only but it touches something instinctive and pleasurable and profitable. And also, crucially, partisan. Part of the delight of belonging to a group is its distinction from another group.

If your dad takes you to watch Manchester United every Saturday of your childhood, you may still never like football. But if you do grow up to like it, it's a racing certainty you'll support Manchester United rather than City. Just as if your mum takes you to mass every Sunday you may still end up atheist. But if you do grow up to get god, the god you get will be the Catholic version rather than the Protestant one that plays at a different stadium. Shankly put that neatly too: 'If Everton were playing at the bottom of my garden, I'd draw the curtains.'

Liverpool, Everton. Manchester City, Manchester United. Catholic, Protestant. Sunni, Shia. England, France. You get little say in your allegiance. And if you think the comparison is far-fetched consider Glasgow, with its two famous football clubs, Rangers and Celtic, one explicitly Protestant, the other Catholic. The line between religious bigotry and sporting rivalry, between parody sectarian war and actual sectarian war, can be so blurred as almost to fade from view.

Sport makes a cracking devotional cause because it has unchanging rituals — the Superbowl, the Stanley Cup, the World Cup, each a festival to look forward to, to build towards, like Easter, like Christmas — yet it is forever self-renewing. Within the ritual framework there is a constant change of cast. New godlets are forever striving to supplant the established gods. Right now there is only one Wayne Rooney, but in days gone by there was only one George Best. The king is dead. Long live the king.

And new thrones are constantly added. The bullshitters have discovered that the formula works more or less regardless of content. I have just, early in the afternoon, flicked through the five dedicated sports channels on Sky TV. One showed golf in the States, one netball, one an interview with a rugby league player, one motor racing and the last one, wonderfully, darts. Fat, pallid, middle-aged white men dressed in what looked like embroidered smocks threw darts at a board. Watching them do so was an animated, engaged, half-drunk, partisan crowd 7000 strong.

Professional sport, then, is a triumphant com-mercial enterprise, generating monstrous sums of money. Its success seems unaffected by global economic problems. It succeeds because it taps into deep-rooted emotional needs: the desire to belong, the craving for a sense of identity, the delight in combat, the urge to worship. It's a winner in every way, a form of entertainment that plays to the fallibilities of the human animal.

But it differs from mere entertainment in one crucial way — the actors are not acting. They are being. They mean what they do. They mean it utterly. The tears of defeat or the grins of victory are never faked. Look at a picture of the All Blacks after they were knocked out of the World Cup in 2007. Their faces are drained, expressionless. They stare unseeing towards a black middle distance, preoccupied with the awfulness of now, unable to escape it. They look like the trench fodder of the First World War, shell-shocked, emotionally wrecked.

It is this intensity, this actuality, that renders sport unique. Despite the frame of bullshit that surrounds it, the weary hyperbole, the mythologizing, the cynical marketing, the proliferation of synthetic competitions, within that frame the strife is genuine. It may be a parody of warfare, but within the sealing bubble of its own rules, it is fought for real. And thus it has jumped what might seem an unjumpable gap. It has become quasi-reality, to such an extent that every news bulletin devotes a segment to it. This fake warfare, this exercise in making money, has achieved almost the same status as actual warfare. Which is like the police investigating a death on *Coronation Street*.

20

Just like us

Because sport has achieved this quasi-actuality, and because it is massively popular, and because it arouses such potent partisan and religious emotion, and because it is seen as a good, other businesses crawl over each other to conflate themselves with it. So even the fat dart throwers wear sponsors' logos. Formula 1 cars are festooned with ads, as are football shirts, rugby jerseys, cricket bats, cricket stumps, cricket umpires even. (The one example of such advertising that I half-admire, if only for its sheer ballsiness, is the sponsorship of a local lawn bowls club by a firm of undertakers.)

Some businesses make use of marginally more sophisticated techniques than conflation. Here's an email I received from New Zealand's second largest company, Telecom. 'Hi, we're massive All Blacks fans and we love to share our passions with you. So, to say thank you for being with us, and to help get you going on XT, we have this almighty AB's offer for you. Upgrade to XT ... and you'll automatically go in the draw to win a once-in-a-lifetime All Blacks experience.'

Telecom want me to transfer my phone to their new network. To encourage me they piggyback on the religious fervour associated with the All Blacks. The adjective 'almighty' comes straight from the prayer book, and the dreary 'once-in-a-lifetime ... experience' suggests a similar absolute. At the same time, by thanking me and offering to 'help get [me] going' they imply that they are acting in my interest. They aren't, obviously, and neither do I expect them to be. They're a commercial business.

But the principal bullshit here is the attempt to personify a commercial entity. They hope to establish a bond with me. They want me to feel kinship. And because as a fifty-something male in New Zealand I am statistically likely to be an All Blacks fan, Telecom portrays itself as one big corporate All Blacks fan.

So I rang 018, the directory enquiry number. I got a charming young man at a call centre in the Philippines.

'What listing, sir?' he said.

I said I'd like a number for the All Blacks.

'One moment, sir,' he said. 'Sorry, sir, we're not getting a direct listing. There's All Black cars, All Black ...'

'Do you know who I mean by the All Blacks?' I said.

'Oh yes, sir,' he said. 'It's the soccer team, right?'

But even if every Telecom employee worshipped daily at the shrine of All Black memorabilia, it would still be irrelevant. Telecom's ostensible devotion to the All Blacks is purely commercial, as is my relationship with Telecom. They run a phone company. I need a phone. I am interested only in the service they offer and the price they charge.

The email is transparently dishonest from start to finish, as hollow as a rotten log. It assumes that I am a thumb-sucking dupe. And yet there is nothing exceptional about its false matiness. Stuff like this bombards us from all sides at all times. Why aren't we screaming?

Air New Zealand, for example, has also hitched its wagon to the emotional engine of rugby. It has painted a plane or two black, it has an on-board safety video starring the All Blacks as flight attendants, and it describes itself on posters and the television screen as a 'fanatical sponsor of the All Blacks'. That phrase implies that the airline is so overwhelmed with its fervour for a rugby team that it signs the sponsorship cheques without even looking at how much of its profits it is casually handing over to the object of its devotion. In other words it's one of us. It doesn't just know how we feel, it actually feels it too. The airline is trying to personify itself.

But Air New Zealand is not fanatical. It can't be, by definition, because an airline is not a human being. For sure the airline is run by human beings, each of whom is capable of feeling fanatical, or indeed of feeling any emotion to which human beings are subject. But Air New Zealand can't because it is just the name given to a business entity.

We tend not to fall in love with business entities. We reserve love for other people and some of the cuddlier species of animal. But business entities would like to be loved, because love doesn't judge. Love is unconditional. Love overlooks faults. And love, as we all know, opens the wallet. So in a bid for our tender affections businesses try to establish themselves as quasi-human beings.

A family with all the ingredients for happiness — looks, nice clothes, a couple of winsome kids — is moving house. The daughter lays claim to her new bedroom and is delighted. She hugs her teddy bear. Then she looks up at the camera and says, in a voice that makes your heart melt, 'Thank you, Mr Hooker.' An invisible choir chirps up to echo the sentiment.

The Mr Hooker in question is L.J. Hooker, the Australian real estate magnate. Born Leslie Joseph Tingyou, he changed his name for fear of anti-Chinese sentiment, adopting the name Hooker either because his father worked as a hooker on the railways, or because hooker was his preferred position on the rugby field. He was later knighted for services to real estate (and I am impressed that I managed to avoid ending that phrase with an exclamation mark). But Mr Hooker had very little to do with the girl's new bedroom because he's dead. His name endures, however, as a real-estate business with franchises throughout Australasia. And to advertise that business they've kept him metaphorically alive to be nauseatingly thanked in person by little girls, because no one thanks a franchise.

Mrs Mac's Famous Meat Pies ('lean meat with a

crusty topping') are sold throughout Australasia. I have just emailed the company that makes them to ask who Mrs Mac is or was. The name suggests a married woman of possibly Scottish heritage, who is known by an affectionate abbreviation of her surname, brought about by the excellence of her baking. There is, as it happens, a stylized bust of her on the wrapper of every pie. She looks suitably sturdy and old-fashioned. You can make out the straps of her apron and her hair appears to be built of sausage rolls.

Mrs Mac's pies are made in Perth, Western Australia. According to the company's website, the factory takes a daily delivery of 14 tons of beef. That's the usable meat from about seventy cattle. Mrs Mac, in other words, deals to the flesh of some 25,000 cattle a year. She's some woman.

(Ah, they've replied to my email already. Sadly Mrs Mac's New Zealand representative is out of office until Friday. If the matter is urgent I can ring him, but I don't think I could justify that.)

That Mrs Mac bakes her pies on an industrial scale does not make them bad pies. But it does make them less emotionally appealing to the pie-eater. Though we consume in vast quantities the products of an industrial age, we don't warm to the notion of industry and industry knows it. So industry does all it can to portray itself as an individual human being, as a sports fan, a home baker, someone fallible and lovable, someone just like us.

I was once invited to speak to some salespeople who worked for ANZ. The bank's current slogan is 'We live in your world'. I didn't thrill to the idea so I quoted a fee that was precisely double the most I had ever been paid for a speech. 'Fine,' said ANZ. The speech went all right and I liked the bankers. Over drinks afterwards I mentioned that I had charged a fee that I considered extortionate and that I was surprised they had agreed to it so readily. 'Mate,' said the manager from the bank that lives in our world, 'we're awash with money.'

21

Oi you

My schoolmate Dave used to play a trick. On a busy street he would lower his head and shout, 'Oi you.' Everyone within earshot would turn to look in our direction. We learned to turn as well, to deflect accusations. When the people turned away, Dave would do it again. Many would turn for a second time, staring with angry suspicion. Dave found it funny. I found it scary. They found it rude and intrusive. And they were right. Yet as citizens we put up with it the whole time.

I reach for the handful of shiny bumf that landed in my letterbox this morning. (Today is Saturday so as a good citizen I am expected to spend it shopping.)

'We have your new outdoor living range.'

'Just what you need.'

'Take your eReader with you everywhere you go, and enjoy reading up to one month on a single charge.'

'Look for this character inside for your chance to win.' (The 'character' is an animated shopping basket.)

'Your local weekly specials.'

'What will you buy with the $2000 you win?'

We are all linguistically programmed to respond to the second person. The reason, obviously enough, is that it addresses us. It is literally personal. But when it is used arbitrarily, when it is thrown out without the speaker knowing who, if anyone, it is reaching, it ceases to be personal. It offers no opportunity to reply and it implies a familiarity with the addressee that doesn't exist. It becomes, in other words, bullshit. The bullshit lies in the illusion of intimacy.

I buy red wine in bulk from the New Zealand Wine Society. The stuff tastes fine to me, it's reasonably priced and crucially they deliver. It's a simple commercial relationship and I am happy with it, but the Wine Society wants us to move on to heavy petting.

'We'd love you to shop with us again,' says a mass-produced brochure, 'so we'll pay the delivery on any wine you buy from the catalogue. We're not offering just anyone this bonus extra, but you deserve it.'

Ignoring the tautology of 'bonus extra', what are the grounds on which my deserving is based? Precisely. There is none. I exist to the New Zealand Wine Society as an account number, as a source of business. My virtues, multiple though they are, are unknown to them. The chances are good that they've sent the same flattering brochure to a serial wife-beater or to a banker from Goldman Sachs.

It is also possible that the wife-beater or the investment banker buys their broadband access from the same company as I do, which is called, for some reason, Snap!. If so, they will have received a brochure on the front page of which there's a close-up of a pair of lips painted orange. Orange is the company colour. The lips are bunched as if on the point of delivering a kiss. The only words on the image, except for the name of the company, are 'We love you'. On the back of the picture, the following text:

Here at Snap! we've been making some big changes. And as a valued customer, we wanted to share them with you first ... we're nice like that. [Pity the big changes didn't include some grammar lessons.]

We're still the same great company with the same great customer service you've come to know and love, but now better than ever! We're sporting a fresh new look and are introducing some really-quite-exciting, fabulous new stuff.

And why would we do all this for you ... well, because we love you!

The correct response would be to drive to Snap!'s offices, burst through the door, seize the first employee regardless of sex, thrust three inches of tongue down their throat and say, 'Right, how about free internet?' But when I pictured the standard internet whizz — name of Greg, keen on gaming, incipient paunch, bad beard, worse shoes — I gave up.

Look at it. Flattery (valued customer), hyperbole (great, fabulous), bragging (great company), unjustified assumption (come to know and love), clichéd paradox (the same but better), the mock-conversational irony (really-quite-exciting), and then the fat demeaning lie of 'We love you'. Where can they have got the idea that we would swallow such transparent bullshit?

Well, Linwood Avenue would be one possibility.

I drove along it this morning. An easterly wind harried the few pedestrians. It flapped the hems of coats, mussed the hair, threatened to flick hats from heads and toss them into the traffic. Grit blew.

While I waited for lights to change I watched a battered woman limp past a billboard. She was an image of endurance. Her ankles were swollen. Her coat and shopping bag looked to date from the 1950s. Wisps of hair had escaped from under her headscarf and whipped around her face. She appeared to be just going on going on, struggling against the wind through a raw urban landscape, bound, I would guess, for some paltry shopping. The huge billboard above her, at which she did not look, said, 'Jesus loves you.'

'Why not give her a car then, Jesus?' I said. Then the lights changed and I drove on.

The billboard is as indiscriminate as the Snap! brochure. It shouts its assertion to all, to passing dogs and cars and shivering nocturnal prostitutes and broken old women battling through the wind to buy a loaf of bread and half a dozen eggs.

We crave intimacy. To be known, to be liked, these things induce a feeling of wellbeing. And to be loved trumps the lot. It stems, no doubt, from Mummy beaming down on us in the cot. Christianity, in all its flavours, and what a lot of them there are, has mined this craving, increasingly so in the last century and a half. It has gradually shifted its sales pitch from promoting a domineering god to a loving one. Less stress on hell (to the point where it is now rarely mentioned) and more on heaven. Less punishment, more personal love. Less dad, more mum. And the second person pronoun is integral to that pitch. It is used to suggest that you are the apple of god's eye.

But it can also be used to suggest you're the prickly pear. Your behaviour can upset god, arouse his wrath. To avoid winding him up you must follow the rules. And the rules begin with 'Thou shalt not'. The god who pronounces 'Thou shalt not' isn't watching over you. He's watching you, with all the sinister connotations of the word. He's the moral policeman. He is the ubiquitous CCTV camera. Not a sparrow falls without your father knowing.

Which is one of the several points where traditional religions and political control coincide. The problem with people is their autonomy. They will tend to do things on their own account, to disobey, to rebel. And it's hard to keep a constant eye over all of them all the time. Secret police are good, but even they can't be everywhere. A fictional rule-enforcer, however, ubiquitous, seeing not only your actions but even into your heart, into your intentions, is the policeman you don't have to pay. Drum him into the mind early and the job is done.

Orwell's 'Big Brother is watching you' is merely a rephrasing of the principle that lies behind all religions, that you cannot escape the all-seeing eye. And it's the second person pronoun that gives the phrase its dread-inducing, boot-in-the-gut quality.

Today that pronoun is forever assailing our eyes and our ears. And if the person addressing us in the second person doesn't know that he or she is addressing us as specific people, is just biffing the word out in the hope that we might take it to mean what it ought to mean, then it is bullshit. The bullshit of the tempter or the bully or the conman, the seeker after power or money.

'Vote National' barked a billboard further down Linwood Avenue, a command in the second person, addressing us in the manner of a sergeant major addressing a squaddie on the parade ground. Like the squaddie we are not expected to bark back, but unlike the squaddie we have entered into no contract where we agree to be barked at, bullied and generally buggered about in exchange for the security and employment of the army. We are autonomous adult human beings going about our private business,

yet we are barked at. And the barker doesn't care
or know who he or she is barking at. He just barks,
perpetually, at anyone, at no one, in the hope that
we'll be mugs.

22

Riding the seesaw of meaning

People like having money. Money in the bank is a buffer against the nasties. It fends them off, or some of them at least, for a while. Money in the bank also represents the potential to buy stuff. And people like buying stuff. If they didn't, there wouldn't be so many shops. Buying stuff, however, entails parting with money. So the decision to buy is difficult. We want to spend our money, but we also want to keep it and we can't do both.

The bullshitter seeks to persuade us that we can.

He wants our money and the power it enshrines so to overcome our understandable reluctance to part with it, he implies that we're not parting with it. He suggests that it is possible to both eat our cake and keep a full cake tin. 'Buy now and save,' he says. He is playing on two meanings of the word save. He is equivocating.

Saving, in the sense of stashing money away, is prudent. It chooses long-term reward over short-term gratification. It is a mature thing to do, the behaviour of a rational adult rather than an impulsive child. So it rightly carries connotations of wisdom and prudence. When the bullshitter uses the word, however, it means something else. It means to fork out less money than you might hypothetically have forked out. But you still conclude the deal with less money than you had before. You have done the precise opposite of saving. The bullshitter relies on the positive connotations of the conventional meaning of the word (prudence, wisdom and gain) being transferred unconsciously onto his radically different meaning of the word.

Equivocation is sleight of tongue. It is comparable to the magician's sleight of hand or the theatre director's use of lighting to manipulate your attention. You can look at only one thing at a time, so magicians and directors draw your attention to the thing they want you to see and away from the thing they don't want you to see. The bullshitter doesn't want you to see the money you will spend. He wants you to see the hypothetical money that you will avoid spending. This hypothetical money is made to feel like a gain. The actual money changes hands off stage. It can be ignored until the bank statement arrives, by which time it is too late.

During the most recent general election campaign the Green Party erected a billboard at the bottom of my street. It featured a boy aged about eight or nine who wasn't quite Maori and who wasn't quite Pakeha, standing in a stream and grinning. (Astonishingly this kid grew a lush moustache within twenty-four hours. Perhaps there was something in the water. Whatever it was also blackened two of his front teeth.) Above the kid's head ran a Green election slogan. 'For a richer New Zealand', it said.

The Greens did not win the election. Few of us voters studied their policies, or indeed the policies of any of the parties, but if asked, most of us would have said that the Greens are idealistic. It would be nice to live sustainably and all that, but economically impractical. Greens, we vaguely believe, would close coal mines, issue no licences to drill for oil, burden farmers and motorists with pollution taxes, and care rather too much for the lumbering whale and rather too little for the sources of wealth. In other words, if the Greens got into power we would be financially worse off. That, regardless of its accuracy, is the perception that kept the Greens vote to 13 per cent or so. It also explains the slogan.

We all know what richer means. It means having more money. And we all know what New Zealand means. It means the people who live here, the voting public. So the self-evident, immediate primary meaning of the slogan is that if you vote Green you'll have more money.

That noise we can both hear right now is the Green party screaming. 'No,' they scream, 'that's not what we mean at all. We're inviting voters to question their values, to ponder the true meaning of richness. Is it richer to have money in the bank or rivers you can swim in? Is it richer to be a nation where everyone has an iPhone or a nation where kids can play safely in asbestos-free meadows, et organically cetera?'

All very clever, but also disingenuous. Had the Greens wanted to say that on their poster, had they wanted to question our enthusiasm for wealth and consumption, they could have done so nice and clearly. But they didn't. They chose to have it both ways. They equivocated.

For us greedy rapists of the environment, richer is about as favourably loaded as it is possible for a word to be. It induces the warmest of feelings in the back pocket. The Greens may say that they mean something different by richer but they are fully aware what it most commonly means. And that primary meaning, the money one, is the one they want to register in voters' skulls in the hope that it will subconsciously do something to invert the perception, the sentiment, that Green policies are more likely to shrink our bank accounts than to swell them.

Equivocation comes in various shades, but all deliberately exploit the ambiguity of words and their emotional connotations. Equivocation abounds in the rhetoric of politics.

For example, we all know what poverty means. The mental image it evokes is Dickensian: kids in rags, workhouse gruel and profound despair. Poverty is nasty. Over the last century or so developed nations have wisely decided that there's enough money to go around and so there's no need for any citizen to suffer Dickensian-style poverty. Hence the welfare state. It decrees a line beyond which no one need fall.

Yet the leader of the opposition Labour Party, David Shearer, has recently stated that, under the current government the number of children living in poverty has increased. Citing figures from the children's commissioner, he asserts that one in five of our kids is now living in poverty. It's a nasty charge, and one likely to enhance the perception that the right wing cares only for its rich mates while allowing the runt end of the population to slide into penury. And if true, it's a legitimate point to raise.

But it depends on how one defines poverty. And it transpires that poverty is now defined as living in a household with an income less than 60 per cent of the median wage. In other words, poverty is no longer the absolute term of Dickensian misery. It has become a relative term.

I don't doubt that Mr Shearer's heart is in the right place, nor do I doubt that it is no fun living off less than 60 per cent of the median income, but nevertheless Mr Shearer is equivocating. He is exploiting the emotive connotations attached to our conventional definition or sense of poverty, while defining it rather differently.

Using this definition, more children may indeed have sunk into poverty under the current government but it does not necessarily mean that they have become poorer. It could also mean that everyone in the country has got richer, including the poor, but that the rich have got richer at a greater rate than the poor have got richer. The poor could still have more money than they had before.

The definition also means that poverty is effectively impossible to eradicate. So if New Zealand discovered vast amounts of mineral wealth and the proceeds were shared around so generously that the median income became $1 million, poverty would still be with us. It would apply to every family earning less than $600,000.

Three days after an earthquake ruined the Christchurch cathedral and many another church in the city, Peter Beck, the cathedral's dean, announced that the quake was not an act of god, that the 'earth was doing what the earth does'. In saying so, Mr Beck was following in a long tradition of ecclesiastical equivocation.

The problem for the clerics has always been how to square the existence of suffering with the existence of a loving creator. It appears to be a contradiction. God loves us and cares for us and he is all powerful. Yet bad things happen to us. The reason it appears contradictory is that it is contradictory. And when two statements contradict each other, one of them must be wrong. Now, there is no disputing that bad things happen to us. Therefore there has to be something false in the notion of an all-powerful god who loves us. Maybe he doesn't love us. Maybe he isn't all powerful. Maybe he isn't there.

But if your life's work is promoting a loving and all-powerful god, none of these conclusions is acceptable. So you have no choice but to equivocate, as Dean Beck did. He can't have it both ways. If god, as it says in the Apostles' Creed, is the maker of the earth, he has the same relationship to it as Fisher & Paykel do to my washing machine. If it malfunctions it's his fault.

A common defence of god is to invoke mystery. God is transcendent and supreme and faultless. We are muddy little earthlings with tiny hopeless brains. It is presumptuous of us even to try to describe his wonder or guess at his purposes. He 'surpasseth all understanding'. So there's an end to your cheeky questions.

God under this definition is beyond definition. He is a remote thingummy about whom we can know or say nothing. He works in mysterious ways his wonders to perform, ways that are unfathomable to us. He is ineffable, which means that he is beyond our capacity to define him in words. All of which is fair enough so long as you stop there. But I've never met a theologian who does stop there. They all without exception go on to describe him in words. They tell you, again without exception, that he is good, and loving, and so on. How do they know? If he is beyond our comprehension he is beyond our comprehension. We cannot know or say anything about him. We cannot know that he is good. He could as easily be bad, or capricious, or forgetful, or a bookcase. We just don't know.

The clerics are seesawing between definitions of a word to suit their purposes. They are equivocating. It is bullshit.

23

Another word for it

The euphemism is as old as language. It originated, I suspect, in superstition. Because it was taboo, or just plain dangerous, to mention gods by name, you substituted some saccharine alternative. The Greeks, for example, referred to the Furies, who were grim avenging female deities, as the Eumenides, or Kindly Ones. The exclamation gosh evolved in a similar way, as did darn it, dang it and blimey.

The most fertile field for euphemism is the political one, and especially when politics gets serious and becomes war. War is messy, bloody and horrible, and unlikely to make leaders popular. So it is understandable that they veil the bad stuff with verbal gauze. The ill-aimed ordnance that blows your own troops to bits becomes friendly fire. The US involvement in the Libyan civil war of 2011 became limited kinetic action. Dead civilians are collateral damage. And holding people under water till they believe they will drown is an enhanced interrogation technique.

Orwell in *1984* famously highlighted the political euphemism. The Secret Police worked for the Ministry of Love. Anything placed in the memory hole went to permanent oblivion. The parodies were founded on a deliberate and absolute inversion of reality. Yet Orwell was barely exaggerating. The newspaper that pumped out the party line for the tyrants of the Soviet Union was called *Pravda*, meaning truth.

Corporations also like to slap on the linguistic make-up. They rarely sack people, but they often downsize, or streamline operations, or rationalize or find synergies going forward. Those who announce the downsizing via a media release are never propagandists. They belong to the communications team or the public relations department.

Yet the curious truth about euphemisms is that if

they work at all they don't do so for long. Consider toilet. Like water closet, or its abbreviation WC, or convenience, or cloakroom (shall we count the cloaks?), or restroom (zzzzz), or comfort room (!), or lavatory, which means washroom, or washroom, or bathroom, it came into being as a way of shying round the nasty truth that we defecate and urinate (and even those latinisms are euphemisms in their way, a form of pseudo-medical distancing). Yet toilet has gradually made the transition from prissy metaphor to direct referent, has come to mean exactly what it was designed to avoid saying, and is now soiled by association. The same is true of all the others. So that today, for example, if an American child tells his mother that he has just been to the bathroom in his pants, Mom knows immediately that the problem is not that he went to the bathroom but that he didn't.

The same thing happens with political and military euphemisms. To execute, in the sense of judicial killing, was once a euphemism. A death warrant was issued and it was the warrant that was executed. But the stark truth of the death could not be smothered. And now the word execute means exactly what it was adopted in order to avoid saying.

In post-Christian Western countries today it is easier to be openly homosexual than at any time or place in history except perhaps ancient Athens. The change has happened quickly. It is easy to forget that homosexuality was decriminalized in Great Britain only in 1968 and in New Zealand as recently as 1986. There remains plenty of hatred but it is shrinking by the year.

The campaign that has made things better began when I was at school. One of its first measures to counter prejudice was to hijack the word gay. This made the use of the word in its established sense effectively impossible. It also rendered many a literary text unteachable. Gay had connotations of cheerful nonchalance, which was of course why it was chosen. The idea was for those positive connotations to settle, like a sprinkle of fairy dust, over the notion of homosexuality. So when people were confronted with homosexuality they would see it as, well, gay.

In one way the ruse worked. Every English speaker now knows that gay means homosexual. But the rest hasn't happened. The original connotations have floated away like that same fairy dust. The connotations borne by the word today merely reflect the attitude of the person using it. So if the speaker is sympathetic to homosexuality he is likely to find the word at worst neutral. But walk into any school playground, and despite decades of sex education and tolerance promotion, you will find that gay is the condemnatory adjective of choice. Anything from a video game to the most virile PE teacher can be just so gay. The revolution has succeeded but the euphemism has failed.

The reason is simple. Words reflect the world. Though constantly and wilfully misused, their eventual tendency is towards the truth. And the truth is that homosexual people are no gayer, i.e. no more nonchalantly cheerful, than any other people. Being homosexual doesn't stop you being misanthropic or splenetic or just plain gloomy. In other words, gays aren't necessarily gay.

So if we agree, as we have, that gay means homosexual, it has to stop meaning cheerful. And if people remain wary of homosexuality, as some do, then gay is going to have negative connotations. Changing the word doesn't change the thing.

I taught at a school where the English department developed an alternative course for the bottom stream. The head of department, tongue partially in cheek, chose to call the course Limpid Writing. It was a good school and a good course and everyone was happy, including the kids. They were under no illusions about the stream they belonged to. Kids never are. But they were pleased to have a new and distinct identity.

They didn't do English: they did Limpid Writing. It said so on the official timetable.

The one trouble was that they were unfamiliar with the word limpid. But they were familiar with the word limpet. So that's the word they used. They referred to the course as limpet writing. The name caught on. In due course the kids took to referring to themselves, cheerfully and quite without irony, as limpets. And everyone else, including the staff, followed their lead.

A limpet is an unimaginative beast. Its idea of intellectual life is to seize a rock and hang on. In other words, limpet is precisely the sort of label that anyone naming a bottom stream would recoil from. The kids remained the bottom stream, of course. And the connotations of bottom stream were transferred in their entirety to the new word limpet, and everything carried on exactly as before. It still makes me smile.

24

Dressing up

Reason is the enemy of bullshit. So bullshit needs to numb reason. One way to do so is to dress up to look like reason.

Here's the text of a television advertisement (though the punctuation is a guess. There is no way to tell from the soothing masculine voice-over where a full stop might come because the words emerge as a warm and unstoppable gush, like velvet vomit. If you are feeling strong you can watch the thing at http://www.youtube.com/watch?v=M-p4azo6aoQ):

Life starts with tears, but that's okay because that's life, so dry those eyes because you don't want to miss a single second of the joy and frustration and passion to come, the second you decide to stay, to go, to call her back, because we love to talk, we need to talk, it's not you it's me but it's not me it's us and we're all right here beside you, so whether … it looks like love or it looks like rain, smile, because life starts with tears but that's okay, that's life, and now you won't miss a single second of it, experience it all on the Smartphone Network.

The text, naturally, is accompanied by images and you can guess their nature — a soft-lit maternity ward, a love-torn woman, a dithering hunk, a smiling taxi-driver, a weeping girl getting into a taxi, sympathetic friends cheering her up, bright umbrellas blooming in the rain, soft-focus images of pretty countryside, Grandpa in a rocking chair smiling at his cell phone.

The distinctive feature of the text is the causal conjunctions 'so' and 'because'. They suggest consecutive thought, the sort of thought that has raised the human being from the swamp of primitivism onto the savannah of enlightenment. But there is no consecutive thought here.

Why is it okay that life starts with tears? Because

'that's life'. It's an intriguing thesis. Whatever happens in this world is okay because it is what happens in this world. Here's the identical reasoning: 'My sister has just been raped by Libyan mercenaries, but that's okay, because that's life.'

It's a circular argument. It begs the question. The reason it gives for everything being okay is that everything is okay. But it looks sufficiently like an argument to have the vague air of wisdom. It also supplies the first ostensible reason for us to 'dry those eyes'. A second reason is that we 'don't want to miss a single second of the joy and frustration and passion to come'.

Well, call me an oddball, but I'd quite like to miss any frustration that's coming my way. (And one head-boiling form of frustration that I could very happily do without is that which surges within me every time I ring Telecom. They have an automated reply system that pretends not to be automated. 'Right,' says a recorded female voice, 'let's see if I can help you. Tell me what you are calling about. You can say things like …' What infuriates me is not just the jaunty tone, nor yet the irrelevance of the questions that the voice biffs at me, nor even the way those questions are designed to discover whether I want to buy some new service in which case I shall be passed instantaneously to a salesperson, but rather the belittling implication that I might fall for it, that I might believe I am talking to an actual sentient human being. It's the implicit contempt that enrages me. Though I have discovered that if you swear viciously at it the system rapidly gives up and passes you on.)

Because appears four times in this ad. But not once does it explain a cause. It just applies a veneer of apparent reasoning to emotive pap. The text combines with the images and the music to solicit a soft and uncritical emotional response, at the end of which we are primed to accept the remarkable instruction to 'experience it all on the Smartphone Network'. How is not made clear.

On YouTube several viewers have written comments on the ad. MegaBrittaney calls it 'inspiring'. Skydive Sabotage 'loves' it. And theharrymclean says 'it is the best telco ad ever'. Sometimes the condemned step cheerfully into the noose and even manage a kind word for the hangman.

The appearance of reasoning is a staple of commercial promotion.

'New Zealand's favourite fruit,' says a well-known former All Black in another television ad, 'and New Zealand's favourite sport.' He then interlocks his enormous hands in the form of a scrum and observes,

'It's a perfect match.' He's plugging bananas. The particular ones he's paid to plug are sold by a vast Californian corporation. The repetition of favourite implies a link between the fruit and rugby. But the link is spurious, as can be illustrated by replacing the word sport with tampon. The form of the apparent reasoning remains unchanged.

Complete the following sentence: 'If you love life, you'll love ...' Our outdoor furniture? This mascara? Bali? The indulgence of a hot-rock, healing-crystal and Ganges river-mud therapeutic massage? All wrong, as it happens, but the point is that all are plausible.

The conditional clause 'if you love life' is designed to generate a yelp of assent. And hoping to piggyback on that yelp is what the bullshitter is trying to foist on his victim. The two clauses are related only grammatically. But what is implied is a logical sequence, if x then y. Such sequences are basic to our understanding of the world. They clarify things. This ad seeks to resemble such a logical sequence while doing the precise opposite. It aims to delude by establishing an unjustified and illogical connection. The thing you will supposedly love, as it happens, is a variety of frozen dessert.

The application of reason leads to science. Science means simply knowledge. We enjoy what it brings into existence but to most of us the science itself is a mystery. We have no idea how drugs work, or televisions, or the electronic mousetrap that sends us a text when it is triggered, but we're grateful for these things and impressed by them. So one of the oldest devices of bullshit is to suggest scienciness.

New Mineral Power healthy perfecting blush by Maybelline offers 'micro-mineral mica' which 'amplifies luminosity'. The vocabulary here is sciency rather than scientific. Mica is indeed a mineral. The micro means only that it's ground up small. I'm not sure that it is possible to amplify luminosity, but both words have the ring of the lab to them.

'New Mineral Power powder foundation is dermo-clinically proven to improve your skin.' These improvements include '50% improvement in luminosity, 40% better skin clarity, 39% reduction in redness'. We are to 'Discover the goodness of micro-minerals in a foundation'. These micro-minerals are 'triple-refined'.

This is pseudo-science. It is carefully pitched to impress while staying on the windy side of the law. 'Skin clarity' is not defined, nor how to measure it. But the precision of 40 per cent and the phrase 'clinically proven' combine to suggest the reassurance of test tubes and bearded boffins in lab coats. They may not be glamorous but they know their stuff.

The whole is a backhanded compliment to the scientific method. It acknowledges that science does good reliable stuff. At the same time it's an implicit insult to its readers, whom it assumes will not know the difference between actual science and the appearance of science, who will be impressed merely by the sound of triple-refined micro-minerals and some unverifiable stats. Falsehood nicking truth's clothes once more.

25

Beat it down, in the name of the father

'Reason,' said Martin Luther, about 500 years ago, 'is the greatest enemy of faith.' He was right. So the church that was founded in his name still does its best to wallop reason on the head, and the key to walloping is to get in early. Here's part of the Lutheran sacrament of baptism.

Do you believe in God, the Father almighty, maker of heaven and earth?

Do you believe in Jesus Christ, His only son, our Lord, who was conceived by the Holy Spirit, and born of the virgin Mary, suffered under Pontius Pilate, was crucified, died and was buried? He descended into hell. On the third day He rose again from the dead. He ascended into heaven and sits at the right hand of the Father. From thence He will come to judge the living and the dead.

Do you believe in the Holy Spirit, the holy catholic Church, the communion of saints, the forgiveness of sins, the resurrection of the body, and the life everlasting?

Following each question, the candidate answers by saying, 'Yes, I believe.' *If the candidate is a child, the godparents are to answer the questions.* (Italics mine.)

Thus they tell the child what it believes before it is capable of speech. They speak on its behalf. They presume on its intelligence. They seek to colonize its brain. They give it a handicap that it will have to overcome, if it is ever to exercise the faculty that distinguishes us from the animal kingdom. They present it with an engrained mental mythology that contradicts all the evidence that will confront it.

They tell it that the dead aren't dead; that rotten flesh comes back to life; that there's a ghost; that there's a place of punishment after you die and a place of reward. All without evidence. All in defiance of reason.

Now it's possible, of course, that all this stuff is true. But if so, you might have thought that a god who was capable of knocking up heaven and earth would also be capable of convincing us of that truth without the intercession of fallible human beings. But no, the kid cannot be allowed to use his power of, presumably god-given, reason because otherwise he might get it wrong. And then he'd fry.

As with all bullshit, the aim is to achieve power over the bullshittee. If you plant this stuff in his or her little head early enough, what can you then not make him or her do? You've installed Big Brother.

Reason seeks answers to questions. Essentially reason moves from the known towards the unknown. You gather the evidence first, the stuff you can show to be true: that, say, the planets move about the night sky in a particular pattern. Then you ask why. The theory you reach must accommodate the evidence. If it doesn't, either the evidence or the theory or both must be false.

The big word is why? As far as we know, the

concept of why is unique to human beings. When children first learn to ask it they can be annoying.

It's time for bed, my darling.

Why?

Because seven o'clock is bedtime.

Why?

Because you need a lot of sleep at your age.

Why?

Well, to be honest my darling, I don't know.

Why?

Look sweetie, go to bed or there won't be any ice cream tomorrow.

Why?

Because I said so.

Why cuts swiftly to the nub of things. And in doing so, why exposes ignorance and bullshit. So it is in the bullshitter's interest to repress why.

One way is to indoctrinate, as illustrated above. A fractionally subtler way is to pretend to share the same spirit of enquiry. Here's the opening of the Shorter Catechism of the Orthodox Presbyterian Church.

Q. 1. *What is the chief end of man?*

A. Man's chief end is to glorify God, and to enjoy him forever.

Q. 2. *What rule hath God given to direct us how we may glorify and enjoy him?*

A. The word of God, which is contained in the scriptures of the Old and New Testaments, is the only rule to direct us how we may glorify and enjoy him.

Q. 3. *What do the scriptures principally teach?*

A. The scriptures principally teach what man is to believe concerning God, and what duty God requires of man.

Q. 4. *What is God?*

A. God is a spirit, infinite, eternal, and unchangeable, in his being, wisdom, power, holiness, justice, goodness and truth.

And so on for 107 questions and answers.

Superficially this looks like human enquiry at work. But it is exactly the opposite. Its sole purpose is not to foster enquiry but to suppress it. The trick lies in the questions. They aren't questions. Questions, by definition, precede answers. But here the answers come first. The only purpose of the questions is to invite a recitation of dogma. The questions resemble the patsies put to a Government minister in Parliament by someone on the same side. 'I'm very glad you asked that,' says the minister and trots out the prepared response.

Only one word is required to cut through this pap: why. Respond to any of these supposed answers, these 'truths', with why, and the Presbyterian church can only answer, 'Because I said so.'

Why?

Because someone said so to me.

Why?

Because they wanted me to believe.

Why?

Because, and so evasively, but revealingly, on.

This catechism, any catechism, aims merely to inculcate a host of unverifiable assertions, dogma that no dog would swallow. And the formula of the catechism is an implicit compliment to the same reasoning faculty that the dogmatists are terrified of and that they are doing all they can to suppress. It's mimicry to avoid predation.

26

All hands to the pump

The *Press* and Linden Leaves are offering all subscribers the chance to win 1 of 16 Linden Leaves Rugby Essentials Sets endorsed by All Black legend, Justin Marshall.'

If you are unfamiliar with the company Linden Leaves you may like to guess what a set of 'rugby essentials' comprises. Boots, perhaps? A ball? A little beer? No. It comprises 'a pump dispenser bottle of fabulous, nourishing shave oil', 'an all over body moisturizer to lock in hydration on a daily basis' and 'a natural exfoliating tube of facial scrub' (and I would be interested to learn what a natural exfoliating tube looks like and where it grows).

Here we have the transfer of expertise (Justin Marshall was a fine half-back but his dermatological qualifications are, I suspect, scant), the pseudo-scientific appeal of 'hydration' and 'exfoliating', the come-on of 'natural' and the effort to yoke cosmetics, somewhat improbably, to the emotional juggernaut of the national rugby team. But there is another technique employed here which is among the most pervasive and corrosive of all. It is verbal inflation.

Though I have no doubt these splendid cosmetics would transform the most grizzled prop forward into a lissom boulevardier with skin as sweet as milk, that still doesn't render them essential. Most rugby players manage to live without them. To describe them as essential debases the currency of language. For if cosmetics are essential, how do you describe food, water and shelter? Essential essentials?

There is similar inflation in the 'fabulous' shave oil. Deriving from fable, the word suggests that ancients sitting round campfires told awe-drenched stories of this shave oil, setting it above and apart from the dull diurnal world. This is a shave oil of mythological status.

Legend belongs to the same word stable. It suggests that Mr Marshall is the distillation of virtues, a hero of tales handed down from generation to generation, refined and simplified by repetition until they enshrine some fundamental truth. He isn't. He's a gutsy half-back from Mataura.

Such inflation, such hyperbole, assails us constantly. Last weekend I was in Rotorua. I spent a morning peering into holes, at the base of which lay steaming, glooping mud. I imagined falling in and dying, lobster-like, boiled by the earth. Here there was no denying that we stand on the thin skin of a cooling planet, a planet that obeys the laws of physics rather than us, that has no interest in our welfare. We have just evolved to occupy a niche in the world it serves up. If the world were different so would we be. If the world changes too quickly for us to adapt, we've had it. Peering into these sulphurous pits induced an agreeable feeling of insignificance. You can't argue with the earth's core. It neither listens nor cares.

Back at my hotel room I found this on the desk. It seemed to come from a different world: 'The buffet is packed with gastronomic sensations and is a feast for the taste buds and the eyes. Enjoy our live interactive cooking station, where you can select your own, personally chosen ingredients, that our talented chef will then cook to perfection.'

It's the standard hyperbole of commerce. We are all familiar with it. We know that the gastronomic sensation will be something nice to eat, that the live interactive cooking station will be a chef at a stove, that the ingredients we select (which will then magically become personally chosen) will consist of meat and vegetables, and that having them cooked to perfection will mean having them cooked. Such translation, such deflation of the verbal bubble, is necessary and, for most of us, effectively automatic.

We are bombarded by absolutes and superlatives. I flick through a few pages of a Sunday magazine. For hair that looks 100 per cent vibrant. Reduce fat and cellulite in no time. Unblemished skin. Perfectly balanced. Five nights of absolute bliss. The merriest Christmas ever. Sheer indulgence. Amazing offer. The ultimate shopping experience. Not to be missed, once-in-a-lifetime, super, huge, massive, unrepeatable, and what does it all mean?

It means heaven. It's the perfectible world, a world born of our sense of time. My dog lacks that sense. Though he is, in his way, a perfect organism, calibrated to fit a niche in the actual world, he accepts things as they are and has no notion of their being better, let alone perfect. He lives only in the present. While his dinner is being assembled he may manage to think a few seconds ahead, and indeed may even try to hurry things along by sitting, but beyond that he has no grasp of the future tense. So he makes no plans. We do.

Our sense of the future enables us to imagine tomorrow being better than today. From there it's an obvious step to trying to make it so. This faculty of imagination has led to all the things from the plough to the internet that have made our lives easier and longer.

The hypothetical end of that urge to make things better is to make them best. We can imagine a point beyond which things couldn't be improved. Thus we conjure the world of Plato's forms, or any of the other names we give to the notion of perfection. And it is into this notion, this sense of how things ought to be, that inflated language dips its greedy beak.

OK! magazine parades a crew of characters, most of them actors on film or television, known to their readers by their first names. 'Brad and Angie's Bedroom Secrets' bellows a headline, blithely ignoring the fact that a secret revealed is no longer a secret. (Not that the secrets amounted to much. Angie revealed that 'she's never been tied up', and that she likes to talk in the bathtub. Brad was less forthcoming.)

Angie and Brad are images rather than people. They occupy a different, better world. And they are venerated because they display all the qualities to which the congregation aspire — fame, wealth, looks and a spectacular, turbulent and vivid love life. They are, in other words, the ideal figures of our age. The gods they most resemble are the pagan crowd of pre-monotheistic times. These gods were far more entertaining than our current versions. They squabbled and shagged, were subject to envy, greed, lust and rage, conducting a sort of divine soap opera. They did what we did but bigger. Ditto the celebs.

Except they don't. Like the squabbling gods, the celebs of the gossip columns are fictional. The actual people whose names they bear, Brad, Angie and so on, are as sublunary dull as the rest of us. As Brad attains his shuddering climax that threatens the joints of the $15 million gold-plated four-poster, and then heaves himself from the quivering fevered loins of the exquisite, though unbound, Angie, I am confident that he, too, wonders quite whether that was it and feels a vague sense of having been duped.

These people are stars. The name is significant. They are celestial beings. They're the conscious creations of an industry founded with adamantine firmness on the potency of bullshit. For since movies began, the power of the camera to create characters who seem to be larger than life has been exploited to tap into our yearning, our hope. It was, from the outset, a deliberate exercise in propaganda, in the manufacture of mythology. And, in the best traditions of myth-manufacture throughout the history of the human species, it has proved hugely profitable.

27

Happy together

Ask children what they want in life and they'll tell you they want to fly helicopters or have a lot of children or drive a Ferrari or live in a mansion or be a fashion model or whatever. Ask them why and they'll look at you oddly. It seems obvious to them. These things will make them happy.

Just about everyone wants to be happy, and it's a reasonable ambition. Happy is nicer than sad. Where the difficulty lies is in identifying and then securing happiness.

We look fondly back on the past and realize, or at least believe, that we were happy then. We look fondly into the future and expect, or at least hope, that we may be happy then. But we tend not to notice whether we are happy in the present tense. For illustration you need only consider the children mentioned above. While describing the things they think will make them happy they would probably grin. And it would be the sort of open and endearing grin that most adults have lost the knack of, even those adults with a lot of children whom they shift from fashion shoot to mansion by Ferrari or helicopter.

Unhappiness is easier. We have no difficulty knowing when we're unhappy and we can generally identify the cause. Being spurned in love, bullied, in a bad job, in a worse marriage, scared, broke, sick, lonely, most of these are easily spotted and sometimes capable of remedy. But happiness and its causes are less easily defined. Happiness, it seems, is like Schrödinger's cat: the moment it's observed it shrivels.

We are skilled, however, in spotting happiness in others. We recognize the symptoms instinctively — the bright eyes, the set of the shoulders, the openness, the smile — and we are drawn to them, because happiness is famously infectious. Indeed, though you rarely hear it acknowledged, one of the commonest causes of happiness is being in the company of happy people. Few of us grin much when alone.

So we crave happiness but are poor at identifying its cause. At the same time we are good at spotting, and attracted by, happiness in others. All of which sets things up nicely for the bullshitter.

In the February 2011 edition of *KiaOra*, the Air New Zealand in-flight magazine, the first ad to feature a human face shows a young man on a beach. He has sunglasses and fine teeth. He is piggybacking a young woman without sunglasses but with similarly fine teeth. I know about the teeth because both the young people are smiling broadly. Their skin is unblemished, the weather glorious, their bowels are under control and predators absent. This couple is happy. A faultless young couple in a faultless world is an image as old as our species. It's the Garden of Eden. Every culture I know of has a similar myth. It enshrines the happiness we think we crave. It is bliss.

The precise cause of the couple's bliss is not made explicit. To the male mind it may seem that they are about to have sex on the beach, which is conveniently deserted. To the female mind it may seem that the two are firmly and joyously bonded. Either way, their situation seems desirable and unclouded by the imperfections that sully our own lives and loves.

Now, which of the following is this image promoting?

A holiday in Fiji?

Tampons?

Toothpaste?

Life insurance?

Household appliances?

Underarm deodorant?

The only one to which the image has any possible relevance is the Fijian holiday. And of course it is not an ad for a Fijian holiday. Nor, as it happens, is it an ad for any of the others. But we could readily imagine it being so. In the land of bullshit, happiness can be and is yoked to anything.

The alternative world that assails our eyes and ears at every turn, that announces itself on billboards, on the television, from the radio, on the pages of newspapers and magazines, abounds in happiness, or at least in its symptoms. It smiles at us constantly. Yet we do not smile back. Look at the faces in the lift, in the street, and especially in the shop, which is the place where most advertising suggests happiness is to be acquired.

In my local supermarket there are posters of produce managers hung on the walls, beaming men and women who love their vegetables, their small goods, their bread, their meat. And, in case we are blind, a celebrity chef booms at us from the public address system, telling us in upbeat and phoney terms about the meals we can cook, the delights in store. The contrast between the tone of the voice and the faces in the checkout queue is comic. It is the gulf between the fantasy and the reality, between a synthetic heaven and an actual earth.

In 1999 Richelle Roberts of California filed a grievance against her employer, the Safeway supermarket chain. Her gripe was the company's 'superior service' policy, and in particular the requirement to 'smile and make eye contact' with every customer. To ensure that the requirement was met, Safeway sent 'mystery shoppers' into their stores. Mystery shoppers means spies.

The problem lies in the word service. Service is courtesy, politeness, attentiveness. It acknowledges a relationship between a buyer and a seller. But smiling and eye contact denote personal interest. 'Some customers mistake our friendliness for flirtation,' said Ms Roberts. Of course they do. Being smiled at makes people feel good. Being smiled at by women makes men feel especially good. And it makes some stupid men believe they are desired.

I have been unable to find the result of the case. I hope Safeway lost. Requiring one's employees to fake the symptoms of happiness indiscriminately is to make a billboard of a human being. (Many people choose to live as billboards, of course, but they are generally paid very well to do so. And they can afford high walls to keep their more honest behaviour from the public eye — though as Tiger Woods and many another celebrity has discovered, it still tends to seep out.)

Helen Clark, New Zealand's prime minister for a decade, is a woman of formidable intellect and undisputed decency. But few would describe her as a byword for joy. The face she presented, to the public at least, was that of the headmistress of one of the more censorious private schools, and her idea of a relaxing holiday was a three-day slog through wet bush. So every three years, as another election loomed, her campaign posters came as something of a shock. Overnight she would appear on the sides of buildings, three times life-size and grinning like a beauty queen. Momentarily it was hard to recognize her.

The happy couple on the beach, by the way, were promoting Hertz, the car rental company. You probably guessed.

28

The tyranny of the image

My dog is running. He has somewhere to go quickly, probably somewhere I don't want him to go. Then a molecule of rotting possum reached the smell receptors in his nose. His muzzle is yanked involuntarily to one side, as if it were moored to the source of the smell. The brakes come on but he is travelling so fast that his hindquarters carry on in the original direction. They swing round, describing a semi-circle, the centre of which is the point to which his nose is now directed. Thus he addresses the smell that he was powerless to resist addressing. The dog is an olfactory creature.

We are visual creatures. It is through the eyes that the stimulus reaches us to prompt a similar and barely resistible reaction. Like music, images bypass the analytical bits of the brain, the critical faculties, and arrow home to the ancient bits. I recall one hot afternoon in Spain when I was riding a bus to a factory where I taught the managers English. Through the bus window I caught a glimpse of a poster so sexy, so precisely attuned to my desires, that I simply got off the bus and walked back to stare at it, powerless to resist the urge. I can still conjure that image in my head, in detail, thirty-three years later. I remember nothing of the lesson I later taught.

A picture is famously worth a thousand words. Time was when every picture had to be made by hand. Now cameras create them endlessly and effortlessly. And no human invention has done more than the camera to enable the proliferation of bullshit.

People who seek publicity design things around the camera. They schedule photo ops. I open today's paper and there is a picture of John Key planting a tree. Only he isn't. He is wearing a suit and the light glints from the blade of his virgin spade. Someone else dug the hole and will fill it back in and tamp it down and mulch and tend the tree. Mr Key is 'planting a tree'. It's a symbol. The image associates the leader with good things.

The fundamental lie of photography is that it freezes time. Consider the Hertz ad. The happy youth is carrying the happy girl across the beach in perpetuity. Their smiles will never fade. Now, I don't recall ever carrying a young woman across a beach, but I can imagine doing so and I am confident that at some point my smile would fade. As I dragged my feet through the sand, stumbling perhaps on a piece of driftwood, or stabbing my sole on a broken shell, I would begin to pant, to sweat. Lactic acid would accumulate in my thighs. And however white the young woman's teeth and however charming her smile, and however her laugh might ring across the sand like the tinkle of silver bells, the time would come when I would say, 'Okay, darling, that was fun, but would you mind getting off? My back's killing me.' In the Hertz ad that time never comes.

Even as amateurs we acknowledge the deceptive potential of the camera. 'Say cheese' says the recorder of the moment. 'Come on, everybody, say cheese.' And we who have stopped having a good time in order that someone should record us appearing to have a good time, dutifully fake it. And when the shutter finally clicks we all smile for real at the relief. But then, ten years later, the photo is all we have of that afternoon and we've grown to believe, gradually, that that's how it was. And when our house catches fire we dash back through the smoke to rescue an album full of such frozen dishonesties. Images are potent.

Because of the potency and emotional immediacy of the image, bullshitters increasingly use words in a manner that strives to imitate its instant appeal. The text of the Hertz ad begins thus: 'Sunny skies. Warm weather. And ways to enjoy even more of it with Hertz.'

Note the sentence fragments, the gobbets of language like patches of colour. No verbs. Nothing complicated. This is language as an emotive anaesthetic. And what it seeks to anaesthetize, as always, is the analytical and critical faculties. What exactly are the 'ways to enjoy even more' warm weather? The next paragraph purports to provide the answer: 'Including a wide selection of vehicles to choose from, 24-Hour access to Emergency Medical and Roadside Assistance plus great additional extras like zero insurance excess and Neverlost GPS.'

Once again we have a sentence with no finite verb. But more significantly this is language divorced from sense. Having '24-Hour access to Emergency Medical

Assistance' is not a way to enjoy more good weather, any more than a zero insurance excess is, or a GPS system. Behind this inanity you can sense a residual trace of what ought to be there. There is in the copy a ghost-memory of the pattern of reasoned argument, but it has been lost in language that aspires to the emotive potency of the image it accompanies.

A century and a half ago an image was a rarity. Today images are impossible to escape. And the most potent purveyor of them by far is that box in the corner of the living room that presents us with a mediated version of the world beyond our walls, the television.

Television has been a worldwide success because, as visual beasts, we absorb the endless succession of images on the screen without interpretative effort. Indeed if a television is on in a room, in a bar, in an airport, it requires a conscious effort not to watch it. The screen is hypnotic, stupefying, infantilizing. It reduces us to the status of babies, lying back and watching stuff moving before our eyes, like the clothesline of plastic shapes stretched across a pram. If the plastic shapes stop moving the baby falls asleep or starts to cry. We just change channel. A simple press of the finger will take us somewhere else in the endlessly entertaining labyrinth of the alternative universe that is tellyland.

The makers of television do not want us to change channel. Their business depends on retaining our attention. So they try never to allow the shapes to stop moving. On the news today there was a story of the possible departure of Greece from the Eurozone. The story told of bailouts, soaring interest rates, a possible run on the banks, all of it significant stuff. But none of it visual stuff. So in order that we baby viewers should not get bored, burst into tears and change channel during an item that lasted a minute at most, we were shown file footage of a machine printing bank notes, hypnotically stacking and slicing, stacking and slicing. Look, said the picture, this is all about money. Look at the clever machine.

29

Branding

I was clever at school and reasonably athletic. But at seventeen and with a late dose of puberty, I didn't want to be clever or athletic. I wanted to be beautiful and cool. I wanted to be Andy. Andy was the coolest kid in our class, with a remote disdain that I revered with such intensity that I thought I was in love with him. But it wasn't so much Andy that I wanted, it was the qualities he embodied.

One Friday evening he turned up at the pub in a V-necked T-shirt with a bird design on it. It made me ache with desire. The following day I toured the shops till I found something similar. There was only one left and it was a size too small but I bought it, and I wore it that evening. Astonishingly it did not make me look cool or beautiful. It made me look like a dork. I wince still at the memory. But in my absurd belief that the shirt would prove somehow magical lies the foundation of much of our contemporary commercial world.

A store in the centre of Milan. At the entrance stand two youths. They are wearing jeans but no shirts. Each youth has the body of a Greek discus thrower. All suggestion of body hair has been waxed or shaved from their gym-buffed muscle. These are ideal specimens of the young male form. Teenage girls mill and titter around them. The youths chat and smile and put their arms around the tittering girls for photographs.

The youths are paid to be there by the store and the store sells clothes. Yet the point of the youths is the clothes they're not wearing. Their job is to embody a muscular ideal that excites girls and arouses admiration or envy in boys. The hope is that these emotions become transferred by association onto the clothes inside the store.

And it seems to be working. The place is

thrumming with the young. Music is playing, music that the young enjoy. Hidden downlights pick out racks of shirts and skirts, and piles of folded T-shirts. Cloth letters are sewn onto the front of the T-shirts. 'ABERCROMBIE & FITCH', they say. The letters are large enough to be read from 20 feet.

At numerous shops nearby there are T-shirts for sale at far lower prices. And since a T-shirt is pretty much a T-shirt, any kids who buy an ABERCROMBIE & FITCH T-shirt must perceive some value in the words. That value cannot be physical because the words don't make it a better or warmer T-shirt. So the value must be psychological. It must also be substantial because the kids are happy not only to pay for it but also to become promotional billboards for it, to announce their allegiance to it, an allegiance legible from 20 feet away. The words ABERCROMBIE & FITCH are that remarkable thing, a brand.

A brand is a cluster of associations. The trade refers to these associations as brand values, but they are not values. They are emotional connotations, the feelings that the brand name triggers in the mind of the purchaser. A successful brand is essentially an irrational, unreflective belief system, a form of juju that turns ordinary objects into sacred objects. So when the teenager fingers an Abercrombie & Fitch

T-shirt it prompts a slew of positive associations that soften the heart and open the wallet, just as Andy's bird-design shirt did for me.

One of the great commercial discoveries of the second half of the twentieth century was that the brand and the product are distinct entities. Take cigarettes, for example. Cigarettes are by and large cigarettes. The differences between them are negligible, the similarities overwhelming. Yet there are a thousand brands.

In the 1970s, when the anti-smoking crusade had just begun and it was becoming harder to say good things about fags, an advertisement appeared in the Sunday magazines. A bird cage hung from a ceiling, lit by a horizontal shaft of light. On the perch, a packet of Benson & Hedges. And on the far wall, the shadow of the cage. On its perch, a budgie. That was it. The ad said nothing about cigarettes, because there's nothing much to say, but it created a surreal image of ironic intelligence. And to this day the notion of Benson & Hedges as a better class of cigarette remains fixed in my skull. For it is in skulls and skulls alone that brands exist. Like cookies in computers.

Nike did not exist when I was a kid. Today they are a huge sportswear company, perhaps best known for their training shoes. Their branding trick has been to associate their gear with an attitude of mind. Nike's most famous slogan, 'Just do it', feels intuitively attractive to our hesitant selves. It evokes decisive derring-do, a devil-may-care commitment to action, let the consequences be what they may. Though as a piece of moral advice its merit does rather depend on what it is you're thinking of doing. Commit rape? Just do it. Bash that little rich kid over the head and steal his Nike trainers? Just do it.

But regardless of its merit as advice, the attitude of mind is spurious. Some training shoes may be better training shoes than other training shoes, but no training shoes have an attitude of mind attached. If you want to just do it you don't need Nike shoes to just do it in, and if you do have Nike shoes they aren't going to just do it for you or make you into a person who just does it. It's self-evident bullshit. But it shifts training shoes.

Interbrand's Top 100 Global Brands report for 2011 judged that the most valuable brand in the world was Coca-Cola. I recently watched a documentary about the manufacture, bottling and distribution of Coke. Approximately two billion servings of Coke are sold around the world every day and the operation of getting it made, bottled and distributed was a wonder of organization, testimony to the unique talents of the human animal to think and design and make and organize and innovate, all of it driven by the remorseless exercise of reason. Meanwhile the process of promoting Coca-Cola, of creating the brand as distinct from the stuff itself, of installing an image of Coke in virtually every skull on the planet, is the apotheosis of bullshit.

Coca-Cola is a sweet fizzy drink with abundant rivals and imitators. When I was a kid one of those rivals, Pepsi, spent millions of dollars trying to demonstrate that most people couldn't tell Coke from Pepsi. They may or may not have been right. But Pepsi were flogging a horse that had long since left for the knackers' yard. They were trying to convince people by rational argument, whereas the decision to choose Coke over Pepsi or any of the other rivals is not a rational one. It's an emotional one, driven by the brand and not the stuff itself. And Coca-Cola leads the world in branding.

Coca-Cola's advertising says nothing about the soda it sells. It aims merely to establish a slew of positive associations that become part of the circuitry of the brain. Once established, that circuitry is there for good, unseen, unacknowledged, unconscious, just available at all times for activation. Obviously the best time to achieve this is when the brain is still forming. So Coca-Cola aims at the young.

To take just one example, it sponsors *American Idol*, a talent show that is hugely popular with teenagers. After each performance three judges comment. It is the moment of the most heightened emotion. And standing on the desk in front of each judge, unremarked but quite unmissable, is a branded Coca-Cola glass. (Coke is not alone, of course, in seeking to indoctrinate the young. McDonald's aims even younger with its Happy Meals and kids' birthday parties. Give me a child till he's seven, and I'll make him love burgers for life.)

Coca-Cola had a good war. Shortly after the States joined the fighting in 1941 the company announced that every serving man should be able to buy a Coke for five cents, regardless of where he might be. Coke bottling plants were shipped all over the world. To the troops the drink became a symbol of their homeland, a patriotic substance, with the warmest possible emotional connotations. And those troops were young men. Most had a further half-century of potential consumption ahead of them.

The ruse also introduced the drink to a plethora of new markets, and in the most propitious circumstances. The Americans were liberators, and Coca-Cola was the American drink. Thus Coke acquired an identity that is effectively political, wedded in the global mind with the notion of American power and American wealth and American freedom. Which is presumably why the Middle East is one of the few regions where it doesn't dominate the soft-drink market. There Coke is outsold three to one by Pepsi, despite Pepsi being every bit as American. In branding, perception is everything.

Coke's slogan writers have always favoured brevity and vacuity: 'Coke is it!' 'Always Coca-Cola.' 'The real thing.' Each of these is an absolute. Each is an assertion. And each is quite unverifiable. Coke simply asserts that these things are so, in the hope that for all their vagueness they will take root. Taken together, the three slogans imply an entity that is eternal, that lies at the heart of things, that endures when ephemera have faded, and that can be defined only in reference to itself. These are substantial claims. But they have been made before and they continue to be made, and not just for Coca-Cola. They apply equally and exactly to god.

I said in the introduction that the bullshitter seeks power over the bullshittee. Power in the end is just power, whatever its specific nature, and its purpose, always and everywhere, is merely to sustain itself, to go on going on. It is Orwell's 'boot stamping on a human face — forever'. The three most common strands of power, which forever overlap and intertwine, are commercial, political and religious. So it is perhaps unsurprising that the world's most powerful brand touches on all three.

30

My sort of pope

Mike visited yesterday with his daughter, whose seventh birthday is next week. I asked her what she'd like for a present. She said she wanted some Sylvanians.

'What are Sylvanians?' I said.

She showed me the website. Sylvanians are families of toy animals with babies. There are cuddly panda twins and squirrel families and piggy triplets, each baby a wide-eyed anthropomorph that comes with a bottle or a cot or whatever. There was page after page of them. The whole collection would cost thousands.

The little girl was staring rapt at the screen. She said she wanted the chocolate Dalmatian twins. I didn't want to stamp on her rapture, but these toys were so obviously cynically designed to arouse her girlish sentiments and thus to plunder Mike's thinly furnished wallet.

I said nothing. She looked at me, and perhaps sensed my distaste. 'But,' she said, 'I can't stop myself saying, "How cute".'

And there you have it. Her instincts were bellowing one thing to her while another part of her self was watching it happen. Here was consciousness at work, self-awareness. And here was a little girl engaged already in what will be a lifelong battle with bullshit.

It has taken me close to a year to write this book. While I've been down here in this basement study my dog has been asleep on the sofa upstairs or stretched in front of the fire. Every couple of hours or so he decides that there might be some chance of getting me to leave the keyboard and play a game or take him out, so he comes padding down the stairs and sits beside me, looking up with brown eyes. I stroke him. He nuzzles against my thigh. I stroke him some more. My chain of thought snaps. And a minute later the dog and I are outside playing tug.

The dog does this because it works. If it didn't he'd stop doing it. As behaviourist B.F. Skinner observed of his lab animals, 'The rat is always right.' In other words the rat, like my dog, acts on sound empirical principles and never fools itself, never believes anything in defiance of the evidence. No animal does. Except us.

Thinkers down the years have not been sanguine about the human ability to identify the truth, or to tell it.

'Everybody lies,' said Mark Twain.

'No one is happy,' said Christian Nestell Bovee, 'without a delusion of some kind.'

'Humankind,' said T.S. Eliot, 'cannot bear very much reality.'

'Man,' said Chekhov, 'is what he believes.'

A belief is an opinion that you cannot demonstrate to be true. Beliefs are worth scrutinizing because that is how we overcome superstition, gain knowledge and make things fairer, more peaceful and easier. But in the end what people believe is their own affair.

Bullshit is an attempt to foist a belief onto others: that these jeans will make you sexy; that when you die you actually don't; that Jews are vermin; that this football match matters. The methods employed to do that foisting are what I have tried to isolate. All of them depend for their success on the nature of human nature, on the muddled condition of the beast that is uniquely self-aware and capable of thinking but that yet remains a beast.

It has just been announced that there is to be a new 'face' for Chanel No. 5, the perfume that famously comprised Marilyn Monroe's entire nocturnal wardrobe. That 'face' is to be Brad Pitt, which is a bit of a surprise. What is less of a surprise is that in exchange for his services, Brad will be paid a six-figure sum (or perhaps it was seven, I can't recall, and it makes no difference to me, and not much to him, really, since he already has enough to last several lifetimes).

But what is most remarkable is the announcement itself. No one has suggested that Brad Pitt likes Chanel No. 5, or uses it. The company is just paying him to act as though he does. And they are telling us so. Here look, they are saying, we've hired a hunk to suck you in. And even though we've forked out heaps we're confident we'll make more money than we're spending because even though we've told you what we're doing, you'll still fall for it.

It's all a bit discouraging.

Alexander Pope, 4 foot 6 inches tall, a lifelong invalid and a hunchback, had this to say about human nature in 1734:

> Plac'd on this isthmus of a middle state,
> A being darkly wise, and rudely great:
> With too much knowledge for the sceptic side,
> With too much weakness for the Stoic's pride,
> He hangs between; in doubt to act, or rest;
> In doubt to deem himself a God, or beast;
> In doubt his mind or body to prefer;
> Born but to die, and reas'ning but to err;
> Alike in ignorance, his reason such,
> Whether he thinks too little or too much:
> Chaos of thought and passion, all confus'd;
> Still by himself abus'd or disabus'd;
> Created half to rise, and half to fall;
> Great lord of all things, yet a prey to all;
> Sole judge of truth, in endless error hurl'd:
> The glory, jest, and riddle of the world!

I first read these lines when I was sixteen years old and I thought them hard to better. I still do.

Celebrity Cat Recipes
(2010)

This book contains neither cats nor recipes, and the only celebrities are on the end of Joe Bennett's skewer: Tiger Woods, say, or Michael Jackson. In this, his thirteenth column collection, Joe brings Billy Bunter into the twenty-first century, marvels at dead American mascots, anatomizes everything from Santa and cockroaches to earwax and Range Rovers, and spends time with that notorious firm of solicitors Mucus, Sputum and Phlegm.

As provocative, witty and cynical as ever, Joe Bennett continues to live up a hill in Lyttelton.

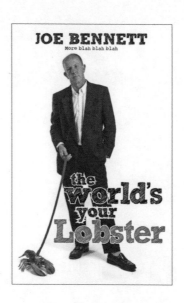

The World's Your Lobster
(2009)

Even by his own rich standards, Joe Bennett's had a remarkable year. New Zealand's foremost columnist has written the inaugural speech for Barack Obama ('Yea, verily, I am come unto you'), given the world a crash course in high finance ('First find your hobo'), watched Christianity play Islam at football, been in court twice (once as Britney Spears), eavesdropped the Pope in Africa, and correctly predicted the skin colour of the Olympics 100-metre champion three weeks before the race was run.

He's given advice to people who're thinking of buying a jogger ('Don't'), written personal ads ('Narcissist seeks similar') and even a poem ('"Tis the day before Christmas and what could be worse, Than having a columnist break into verse?'), and all in all he's done his best to shine light on a naughty world with language as fresh as a virgin's breath.

Joe still lives in Lyttelton. He has a house on the hill and a study with no windows.

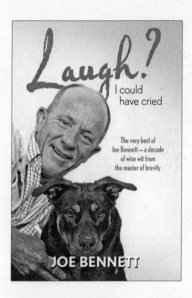

Laugh! I Could Have Cried
(2008)

Joe Bennett was born into the middle classes of England in 1957. Life was stable, suburban and sunny. Computers weren't around to ruin his childhood, nor terror of paedophiles, nor fast food. He had it easy.

Aged twenty-nine, he came to New Zealand for one year to teach. Aged fifty-one, he's still here. But in 1998 he swapped the classroom for the opinion page of the nation's newspapers. Since then, Joe Bennett has been Qantas Media Awards Columnist of the Year three times, he's had eleven collections of his columns published in New Zealand and three worldwide, he's written three best-selling travel books, he's become a regular on radio and television, and he has made far too many after-dinner speeches.

In the introduction to his very first collection, Joe Bennett wrote: 'If anything holds these articles together it is that I like people but not in herds. I distrust all belief, most thought and anything ending in ism. Most opinion is emotion in fancy dress.'

Ten years later, this book presents the very best of a decade's work, organized by topic. Here are his most memorable thoughts on dogs, games, language, travel, the idiocy of belief, and the swamping trivia that shape our lives despite our best intentions, all of them written with the ferocious comic clarity that has made his name.

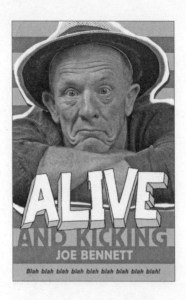

Blah blah blah blah blah blah blah blah blah!

Alive and Kicking
(2008)

Alive: aboveground, animate, animated, breathing, bright-eyed and bushy-tailed, capable of life, chipper, conscious, endowed with life, enjoying health, enlivened, eupeptic, existent, fine, fit, fit and fine, full of beans, healthful, healthy, in condition, in fine fettle, in fine whack, in good case, in good health, in good shape, in health, in high feather, in mint condition, in shape, in the flesh, in the pink, inspirited, instinct with life, live, living, long-lived, quick, tenacious of life, very much alive, viable, vital, vivified, zoetic.

Kicking: sticking the boot in.

Still alive after eleven years and eleven collections of columns, Joe Bennett sticks the boot into Beckhamania, golf umbrellas, beer ads, Hillary Clinton, all sorts of bureaucrats, and a fatso from the Middle East who flies halfway round the world to shoot our deer. But he writes loving stuff, too, about fish and postcards and Pavarotti and butter and dead dogs.

From his fastness in Lyttelton, New Zealand's best-loved columnist once again dissects the weird, wide and sometimes less than wonderful world with peerless wit and concision.

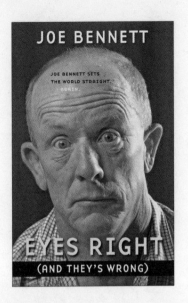

Eyes Right (and They's Wrong)
(2007)

In the last year New Zealand's favourite columnist has turned fifty, lost a dog, been to China, been motivationally spoken to, built a goatshed, drunk with a Bangkok Buddhist, survived Christmas, eavesdropped Winnie with Condoleezza and … but why not let him tell you about it himself? *Eyes Right (and They's Wrong)* is Joe Bennett at his ruthless, funniest best. There's no more to say, really.

He continues to live in Lyttelton. Just.